FOR THE GRANDCHILDREN

A Collection of Stories, Life Lessons, and Wisdom from Around the World

Volume I

Dawn James, along with:

Klaus Armstrong-Braun, Caroline Barrow, Christine Bode, Annette Eberhart, Sharon Kamassah, Oluyinka Marcus, Dr. Tiney Ray, Sean Robinson, Moji Taiwo, Andrea Wardsworth Beasley

Publish and Promote

Published in Canada by Publish and Promote

FOR THE GRANDCHILDREN BOOK SERIES
A Collection of Stories, Life Lessons, and Wisdom from Around the World
Volume I

Paperback ISBN: 978-1-998544-00-4
E-book ISBN: 978-1-998544-01-1
Hardcover ISBN: 978-1-998544-02-8

Book Production by Dawn James, Publish and Promote
Edited by Christine Bode, Bodacious Copy
Interior layout and design by Perseus Design
www.publishandpromote.ca
www.forthegrandchildren.org

Printed and bound in Canada

Note to the reader: The events in this book are based on the writers' memories from their perspective. Certain names have been changed to protect the identity of those mentioned. The information is provided for educational purposes only. In the event you use any of the information in this book for yourself, which is your constitutional right, the author and publisher assume no responsibility for your actions.

FOR THE
GRANDCHILDREN

"The greatest untapped resource is the collective wisdom of our elders."

~ Anonymous

Dedication

This book is dedicated to the elders who have walked this journey before us and to the generations yet to come. We can bridge the past to the future by preserving and sharing our stories, dreams, hopes, trials, triumphs, and wisdom.

Contents

Preface

One story can melt our hearts. One book can change the trajectory of our lives.

How the *For the Grandchildren* book series came to be is a bittersweet story. A few years ago, I lost five elders in our family within eighteen months. During the process of grieving, my neighbour lent me a book called *All We Can Save: Truth, Courage, and Solutions for the Climate Crisis.*

Little did I know that reading this book would light up my soul with the notion that—**we need to save Elder Wisdom.** I reflected on the stories my elders had told me over the decades and all the rich life lessons they had poured into me—those stories were priceless! I set out on a quest to collect, preserve, and share Elder Wisdom with the grandchildren of today and tomorrow.

Why do I call the series *For the Grandchildren*?

Even if you are not or have never been a parent or a grandparent, the one thing everyone on this planet has in common is that **we are all grandchildren**. As such, the *For the Grandchildren* book series is for everyone to read, enjoy, and be inspired.

Dawn James,
Anthologist, Director of Publish and Promote, Founder of FortheGrandchildren.org

Introduction

Do you remember your grandparents' names? What about the names of your great-grandparents? Do you know where they were born, where they travelled, what their talents were, and what challenges they overcame?

The stories of our elders are powerful. Even if we have heard the stories many times before, they seem to stir something within our souls. Hearing stories of adventure, resilience, courage, and achievement makes us feel proud and gives us strength.

Sadly, these stories are all too often lost when an elder passes away, and all those benefits of telling our stories disappear, too.

I believe we can make a difference in the lives of many by sharing Elder Wisdom stories from around the world.

In our inaugural book in the series ***For the Grandchildren: A Collection of Stories, Life Lessons, and Wisdom from Around the World,*** we have a diverse group of people from Canada, the United States of America, Africa, Europe, and the Caribbean sharing stories such as:

- What it means to be a grandparent
- Remembering loved ones
- Knowing your worth
- How to cultivate skills for social and financial success
- Embracing our perfect imperfections
- How to turn challenges into opportunities
- The value of education and lifelong learning
- Planting seeds to feed your mind, body, and spirit
- The importance of showing up, speaking up, and fulfilling your calling
- And becoming the best version of yourself despite harsh beginnings

By sharing these stories, we hope to increase humanity's capacity for understanding, compassion, and inclusiveness.

As you read these stories, we hope you will be inspired and motivated to become the *best and wisest version of yourself*!

Guiding Lights: The Power of Resilience, Integrity, and Lifelong Learning

Tiney Ray PhD, DNP, FNP, PMHNP-BC

Imagine standing at the edge of a vast, uncharted territory filled with winding paths, towering mountains, and hidden valleys. This is the journey of life, an adventure each of us embarks upon with a heart full of dreams and a mind brimming with questions. As you read these words, think of them as a map drawn from the experiences and lessons of someone who has walked many miles on this path before you. This map isn't just a guide for surviving the journey but a blueprint for thriving, finding joy and fulfillment even in the most challenging terrains.

Life is an intricate dance of experiences, each step teaching us something new about ourselves and the world around us. Every twist and turn, every high and low, contributes to the mosaic of our existence. This journey is not merely about reaching a destination but about embracing the process, learning, growing, and finding meaning in every moment.

Key Point 1: The Power of Resilience

Life wasn't always easy growing up in the Bronx, New York. The streets were filled with challenges, much like the rocky paths that make a journey difficult. But amidst these hardships, there were also gifts that sparked my imagination and fueled my resilience. My father, a man of great wisdom, gave me an encyclopedia set and a chalkboard. These gifts were gateways to worlds beyond my immediate surroundings, allowing me to grow and flourish despite harsh conditions.

Resilience is like a seed planted in concrete, pushing through the cracks to reach the sunlight. For me, education was a way to grow despite the difficulties. The encyclopedia and chalkboard became tools for exploration and learning, offering stability and hope during times of abuse, neglect, and even homelessness. Reading allowed me to escape and live vicariously through characters who faced their own trials and triumphs, teaching me that resilience isn't just about enduring hardship but about finding strength and inspiration amidst it.

As a young mother without substantial role models, I faced the daunting task of parenting. My early experiences and flawed decisions could have trapped me in a cycle of hardship. But resilience is like a river—ever-flowing, finding new paths. Determined to provide a better life for my child, I sought further education and certifications, moving away from public assistance towards self-sufficiency. Resilience, I learned, is about forging ahead with a renewed sense of purpose, transforming pain into power, and obstacles into opportunities.

Resilience also involves adaptability, a willingness to change and grow in the face of new circumstances. Each setback became a stepping stone, each challenge an opportunity to develop new strengths and insights. This mindset allowed me to approach life with a sense of optimism and hope, knowing that every obstacle could be overcome with determination and perseverance.

Key Point 2: The Importance of Integrity

Integrity is like a lighthouse standing tall on a rugged coastline, its light unwavering amidst the fiercest storms. Growing up in a devout family and attending Catholic school, I was taught the significance of honesty and moral courage from a young age. However, the real test of these teachings came during difficult periods in my life. As a young mother, I faced numerous temptations to cut corners and take easier routes. However, I realized that true success comes from unwavering integrity.

Integrity is like a compass in life. It ensures that you are moving in the right direction, even when the path is steep and fraught with obstacles. This lesson became particularly clear during my journey through love and marriage. My first marriage, driven more by societal expectations than genuine understanding or love, taught me the importance of making decisions that align with one's true self and values. Years later, when true love found me, I approached the relationship with honesty and authenticity, sustaining our bond for over twenty-seven years.

Integrity also played a crucial role in my professional life. As I pursued further education and moved away from public assistance, I encountered numerous opportunities to take easier, less ethical paths. Yet, I chose to adhere to my principles, knowing that true success and respect come from doing the right thing, even when it's difficult. This commitment to integrity earned me trust and opened doors that would have remained closed otherwise.

Integrity extends beyond personal relationships and professional life; it is the foundation upon which a meaningful and fulfilling life is built. It is about being true to oneself and one's values, even when no one is watching. It is about making choices that reflect our deepest beliefs and maintaining consistency between our words and actions.

Key Point 3: The Role of Humility

Humility is the fertile soil where all virtues grow, forming the foundation for personal growth, learning, and meaningful relationships. As a young mother striving for a better future, I learned that true strength lies in acknowledging limitations and seeking help when needed.

Humility is like climbing a mountain; even the strongest climbers sometimes need support. This mindset helped me reach out to mentors and peers, learn from their experiences, and grow stronger. In my spiritual journey, humility led to a compassionate understanding of God's nature, emphasizing love and forgiveness over judgment.

In parenting, humility allowed me to guide my child with love and empathy. Admitting I didn't have all the answers and learning from past mistakes made me more compassionate. This approach strengthened our bond and fostered an environment where my child felt supported and valued.

Professionally, humility meant being open to continuous learning and growth. Despite achieving various certifications, I remained receptive to feedback and new perspectives, enabling me to adapt to changes and collaborate effectively with colleagues and students. This taught me that leadership is about serving others and fostering their growth, not asserting dominance.

Humility is intrinsically linked to gratitude. I cultivated contentment and peace by appreciating others' contributions and the blessings in my life. This attitude of gratitude became a source of strength during challenging times, reminding me of the support systems and opportunities that facilitated my progress.

Through humility, I have learned the importance of seeking help, valuing others' contributions, and continuously growing. This principle has been essential in my personal, spiritual, and professional life, helping me build meaningful relationships and achieve lasting growth.

Key Point 4: The Strength of Faith

Faith is like a mighty oak tree, standing tall and unyielding amidst the fiercest storms, with deep roots providing stability and strength. My early experiences with faith were shaped by a devout upbringing and education in Catholic schools. However, significant life challenges evolved my understanding of faith.

Faith is about a personal, intimate connection with the divine, finding strength and solace in the belief that a higher purpose guides us, even when the path is unclear. Faith illuminated my way forward during my darkest times, providing the courage to take the next step, even when the future seemed uncertain.

One profound moment of faith occurred at my lowest point, struggling to provide for my child and feeling overwhelmed by my circumstances. In a quiet moment of prayer, a profound sense of peace and reassurance washed over me, as if God was gently reminding me that I was not alone. This experience reinforced my belief that faith is about seeking answers and finding comfort in the divine presence amidst uncertainty.

Faith also played a crucial role in my relationships, helping me find the strength to forgive, heal, and remain open to love. My first marriage, though challenging and ending in divorce, taught me valuable lessons about love and commitment. Through faith, I found the strength to forgive, heal, and stay open to love. Years later, when I reconnected with my true-blue companion, our relationship, built on mutual faith and respect, has been a source of strength and joy for over twenty-seven years.

Faith has guided my spiritual growth. Shifting from a punitive view of God to one of unconditional love and forgiveness transformed how I approached life's challenges. Faith taught me that it is not about fear but trust and surrender, viewing difficulties as opportunities for growth and deeper understanding.

Key Point 5: The Power of Accountability

Accountability is like a captain navigating a ship across vast, unpredictable seas. Every decision impacts your journey and the lives of those aboard. Accountability has been a cornerstone in my life, helping me navigate personal and professional relationships.

Accountability is like a gardener tending to a garden, ensuring each plant receives the attention it needs to flourish. In parenting, this meant acknowledging my mistakes, learning from them, and setting a positive example for my child. In my professional journey, accountability required me to hold myself responsible for my commitments, ensuring each task was performed with care and integrity.

At times, I struggled with past decisions, feeling burdened by guilt and regret. Through accountability, I found a path to self-forgiveness and improvement. By acknowledging my flaws and working to rectify them, I improved my circumstances and set a positive example for my child.

Accountability played a vital role in my professional journey. As I pursued further education and moved away from public assistance, I encountered numerous challenges that tested my resolve. Each step forward required me to hold myself accountable for my commitments, whether completing assignments, meeting professional standards, or maintaining ethical practices.

Accountability has been the glue that holds bonds in my personal relationships. It means being honest about my shortcomings and making amends when necessary. This practice has strengthened my relationships, creating a foundation of trust and respect.

As you embark on your journey, let accountability be your guiding star. Embrace it as a principle that shapes your decisions and actions, ensuring you live a life of integrity and respect. Remember, your actions influence the trajectory of your life and those around you. Accountability empowers you to make choices that align with your values and build a legacy of trust and respect.

Key Point 6: The Joy of Lifelong Learning

Lifelong learning is like a tree that grows and flourishes, constantly reaching for the sky. From a young age, my father instilled in me a love for learning. This mindset has been a source of strength and resilience, helping me navigate life with curiosity and optimism.

Lifelong learning is like a river, evolving and adapting to new challenges and opportunities. It encompasses all forms of personal and professional development, encouraging continuous improvement and growth.

Pursuing further education provided a way forward when I felt overwhelmed by young motherhood and financial instability. Enrolling in courses and obtaining certifications opened new career opportunities and empowered me with a sense of accomplishment. One memorable teaching experience involved helping a struggling student understand the material through new approaches, reinforcing that learning is collaborative and dynamic.

Lifelong learning has also been a cornerstone of my personal growth. Facing challenges in relationships, parenting, and spirituality, I turned to books, mentors, and self-reflection. This quest for knowledge deepened my empathy and broadened my horizons.

Embrace the joy of lifelong learning. It keeps us vibrant and resilient, empowering us to adapt, overcome obstacles, and seize opportunities. Let lifelong learning enrich your journey and illuminate your path to success.

Key Point 7: Embracing Change and Adaptability

Adaptability is like a chameleon changing its colour to thrive in diverse environments. Embracing change and cultivating adaptability have been essential in navigating personal and professional challenges. Each step in my journey demanded flexibility and a willingness to embrace the unknown.

In the early stages of my career and personal life, I often faced situations that required swift adjustments and new approaches. The transition from a young single mother struggling to make ends meet to an educated professional was marked by numerous changes. Each step demanded flexibility and a willingness to embrace the unknown.

Imagine a sailor navigating the open sea, constantly adjusting the sails to harness the wind's power and steer the ship toward its destination. This metaphor captures the essence of adaptability—adjusting our approach to life's unpredictable winds while staying focused on our goals. Embracing change has allowed me to turn potential setbacks into opportunities for growth and development.

A pivotal moment in my journey was my decision to pursue further education. This decision required a significant shift in my routine and priorities, balancing the demands of parenting, work, and studies. It was a challenging period, but it taught me the importance of being adaptable and open to new possibilities. The skills and knowledge I gained during this time advanced my career and enriched my personal life, providing me with the confidence to face future challenges.

Adaptability is not just about responding to change; it's about anticipating it and proactively preparing for it. Imagine a chess player always thinking several moves ahead, considering various scenarios and planning strategies accordingly. This mindset has been crucial in my professional life, particularly in the ever-evolving field of education. Staying ahead of trends, embracing new technologies, and continuously refining my teaching methods have been vital in providing the best possible education to my students.

There was a time when a major shift in educational standards required me to overhaul my curriculum and teaching strategies. Rather than resist the change, I saw it as an opportunity to innovate and improve. Collaborating with colleagues, attending workshops, and engaging with new teaching tools allowed me to create a more dynamic and effective learning environment. This experience reinforced the value of adaptability, demonstrating how it can lead to positive outcomes even in the face of uncertainty.

In my personal life, adaptability has been equally important. Relationships, parenting, and personal growth require a flexible approach, as each stage of life brings new challenges and opportunities. Imagine a gardener who adjusts their care techniques based on the seasons, ensuring each plant thrives under varying conditions. This adaptability has helped me nurture and maintain meaningful relationships, adapt to my children's evolving needs, and continue growing as an individual.

One of the most significant lessons I've learned is that change is inevitable, and our ability to adapt determines our success and happiness. Embracing change with a positive attitude and a willingness to learn can transform potential obstacles into stepping stones. This perspective has allowed me to navigate life's uncertainties with resilience and optimism, continually evolving and growing stronger.

As you embark on your journey, remember that adaptability is a powerful tool. Embrace change as an opportunity for growth and cultivate a mindset open to new possibilities. Let the chameleon be your guide, demonstrating the beauty of flexibility and the strength found in adaptability.

In a constantly changing world, your ability to adapt will be critical to your success and fulfillment. Whether in your career, personal relationships, or personal development, embracing change positively and proactively will enable you to navigate challenges confidently and gracefully.

Let adaptability be the wind in your sails, propelling you forward. With this principle guiding you, you'll be able to harness the power of change, turning uncertainties into opportunities and building a resilient, dynamic, and deeply fulfilling life.

Key Point 8: The Power of Community and Relationships

Community and relationships are like a tapestry, each thread contributing to a beautiful design. From a young age, I experienced the profound impact of community, growing up in a close-knit neighbourhood in the Bronx. This sense of belonging and mutual support taught me that we are stronger together.

Community and relationships provide us with strength, guidance, and the ability to achieve more than we ever could alone. Building solid relationships with colleagues and students has been a cornerstone of my success as an educator. These connections have provided a sense of purpose, joy, and resilience.

One of the most significant experiences that highlighted the power of community was during a period of financial hardship and homelessness. During this challenging time, the support of friends, family, and community organizations provided the resources and encouragement I needed to get back on my feet. Their kindness and generosity reinforced the importance of giving back and being an active, supportive member of my community.

Building strong relationships with colleagues and students has been essential in my professional life. Imagine a garden where each plant thrives because of the careful nurturing and collaboration of the gardener and the elements. This metaphor illustrates how cultivating positive relationships in the workplace creates an environment where everyone can flourish. We can create a supportive and collaborative atmosphere that enhances learning and growth by fostering a sense of community.

One memorable example from my teaching career involved organizing a community service project with my students. Working together to address local needs, we positively impacted our community, strengthened our bonds and developed a deeper understanding of the value of teamwork and mutual support. This experience highlighted how community engagement enriches our lives and fosters a sense of purpose and connection.

Relationships are equally important in our personal lives. The love and support of family and friends provide us with a safety net during tough times and a source of joy and fulfillment during good times. Consider a tree with deep roots and branches that reach out, providing shelter and sustenance. This tree symbolizes the relationships that ground us and nourish our spirits, helping us to grow and thrive.

Maintaining strong relationships with my children, spouse, and extended family has been a priority throughout my life. These connections have provided me with a sense of purpose, joy, and resilience. They have taught me the importance of communication, empathy, and unconditional love. In times of hardship, these relationships have given me the strength to persevere and the motivation to strive for a better future.

As you navigate your journey, recognize the power of community and the importance of building and nurturing relationships. Surround yourself with people who support and inspire you, and be a source of support and inspiration for others. Engage with your community, contribute to its well-being, and foster a sense of belonging and mutual respect.

Let the tapestry of community and relationships be the backdrop of your life, weaving together diverse threads of experiences, perspectives, and connections. This rich fabric will provide you with strength, resilience, and a profound sense of purpose and belonging.

In a world that can sometimes feel fragmented and isolating, the power of community and relationships is a beacon of hope and connection. Embrace this principle and let it guide you toward a life filled with meaningful connections, mutual support, and collective growth. By doing so, you'll not only enrich your own life but also contribute to a more vital, more compassionate world.

Conclusion: Embracing Life with Resilience, Faith, and Lifelong Learning

Reflecting on my journey from a young girl in the Bronx to an educator, medical clinician, and lifelong learner, I realize that integrity, humility, and spiritual growth have been my guiding stars. These principles have helped me overcome adversities and enriched my life, providing a sense of purpose and fulfillment.

Imagine life as a tapestry, each thread representing a lesson learned, a challenge overcome, a moment cherished. The richness of this tapestry is defined by our experiences and the values we hold dear. By embracing these principles, you add vibrant colours and intricate patterns to your life's tapestry, creating a masterpiece that tells your unique story.

Throughout my life, resilience has been a cornerstone. Just like a tree bending with the wind yet remaining rooted, resilience allows us to withstand life's storms and emerge stronger. It's about facing difficulties with a positive mindset, learning from setbacks, and continually moving forward. This strength is about enduring hardships and thriving amidst them, finding light even in the darkest times.

Faith has been my anchor, providing unwavering support and guidance. It has taught me that even when the path is unclear, trust in a higher power can lead us to where we need to be. Embracing faith with an open heart and a curious mind allows us to see beyond immediate challenges and understand that each experience is part of a greater plan.

The river metaphor illustrates that lifelong learning is the continuous flow that nurtures our growth. It's about remaining curious, seeking new knowledge, and embracing opportunities to expand our horizons. This commitment to learning keeps us relevant in a changing world and enriches our lives, fostering personal and professional growth.

As you journey through life, remember these guiding principles. Embrace resilience in the face of adversity, allowing it to strengthen and shape you. Nurture your faith, letting it guide your actions and decisions with love and compassion. Commit to lifelong learning and let curiosity lead you to new discoveries and deeper understanding.

Imagine yourself as a navigator on a vast ocean with these principles as your compass. They will help you steer through turbulent waters and calm seas alike, ensuring you stay on course toward a fulfilling and meaningful life.

In closing, I leave you with this: Live with an open heart, a curious mind, and steadfast faith. Be true to yourself, be accountable for your actions, and continuously seek knowledge. These values will help you overcome life's challenges and enrich your journey, making it one of purpose, joy, and significance.

This is the legacy I hope to pass on to you—a blueprint for living a life of integrity, growth, and fulfillment. May you navigate your path with grace and courage, always guided by these enduring principles. Let your life's tapestry be rich with the colours of resilience, faith, lifelong learning, and the strength of community and relationships.

Embrace each moment, learn from every experience, and let these guiding lights lead you to a future filled with boundless possibilities. Your journey is unique, and your potential is limitless. With these principles as your foundation, you can build a life that achieves your dreams and inspires others to follow their paths with hope and determination.

ABOUT DR. TINEY RAY

With over thirty years of experience in the healthcare field, Dr. Tiney Ray is the founder and owner of Lyght Bulb Moment Foundation Inc. and Lyght Bulb Moments LLC and the co-owner of Telemedicine Essentials of America. Her extensive background includes serving as a certified dementia practitioner and nurse practitioner specializing in dementia care.

Dr. Ray is dedicated to educating and supporting families and healthcare organizations in implementing research-based practices for all stages of dementia. Through her work, she assists in creating individualized care plans that enhance the quality of life for those affected by dementia. As the Lead Dementia Specialist at Biscochito, she is committed to transforming the care experience for older adults.

In addition to her work with dementia patients and their caregivers, Dr. Ray has a strong passion for community public health. She focuses specifically on mental health, substance abuse, and providing a safe, holistic environment for people to heal.

For more information, please visit the website:
Lyght Bulb Moments, https://lyghtbulbmoments.com

Life From a Faraway Place

Moji Taiwo

It was midweek on a beautiful, sunny afternoon in a faraway place when a beautiful olive-skinned baby with a headful of curly, soft hair and unusually light-brown, clear eyes was born in 1958 into a large family of six children. She became the seventh child, and five years later, her baby sister arrived to complete the family of eight children, a father and mother, an uncle and aunt with cousins and extended relatives. The home front was always abuzz. That child was me!

I was born into a mixed family of eight children, with me being child number seven. I have three older sisters, three older brothers and one younger sister. My older sisters and one older brother are from my mother's previous relations, while two of my older brothers, younger sister, and I share the same mother and father. There is a seventeen-year age gap between me and my eldest sister and a five-year gap between me and my younger sister, which means my oldest sister is twenty-two years older than her youngest sister! Therefore, I was a child born to older, loving, and caring parents!

All of us shared a one-room living quarter with intermittent reprieves provided by the older siblings. Three older sisters got married to create space for us younger ones, and my brothers went away to either live with relatives or move on to boarding schools away from home to further their high school education.

I should mention here that my older sisters received minimal formal education and opted for marriage as an escape from home due to a lack of belief or encouragement about educating female children in that era. My mother would have loved to have her daughters educated; however, as is commonly practiced in African countries, fathers hold the final say in decisions pertaining to children. Therefore, my sister missed a crucial formative life development. Fortunately, my father was a rare, progressive African man who encouraged formal and higher education for all his children. As a result, all my brothers, myself, and my younger sister hold at least a bachelor's degree.

Most homes built in Nigeria during the time I was born had a communal plan. Different rooms opened into a commonly used compound, kitchen, and two bathrooms, comprised of two toilet stalls and two shower stalls. It was communal living on a grand scale, which benefitted us as children because there were always aunts, uncles, cousins, and neighbours to play with and people to look out for us. However, there was no privacy, and everybody knew everyone's business. The only private place for my family and me was our one bedroom, which we used only when dressing and sleeping! We also lived with our extended family members, non-relatives, and tenants in the same household for years.

We had no car, telephone, or television. Still, someone in the compound always had a transistor (portable) radio we hurdled around to listen to news, current affairs, and the latest music on the airwaves. Music from faraway places in Europe, America, and other parts of Africa. Music from the USA and England especially.

As you can imagine by now, we were living amongst people of all ages and characters. We learned to share our limited resources, looked out for each other and co-habituated as peacefully as possible. I did not have to wait for my mother to arrive home before I ate in those days, and there was no shortage of teachers, caregivers, mentors, and disciplinarians; a village was raising us. Hence, the African proverb, "It takes a village to raise a child."

I grew up in the metropolitan city of Lagos (specifically, Lagos Island), Lagos State, Nigeria, West Africa. Lagos is a major financial centre in Africa, and it represents the economic hub of Nigeria, which has considerable influence on commerce, entertainment, politics, technology, education, arts, and fashion. As of 2023, Wikipedia reported that the population of Lagos State is approximately 16,000,000 people compared to 762,000 people in 1960 when I was just two years old. Even then, Lagos was a thriving, bustling, fast-paced, developing urban community. However, only affluent houses in my neighbourhood had televisions with black and white pictures, running (tap) water, flushed toilets, and refuse disposal.

Because my mother was determined to raise an educated girl child and because of my father's insight into the socio-economic benefits of education, my childhood consisted of self-discipline, hard work, focus, resiliency, integrity, and a sense of community service.

Although I was born into an Islamic faith family, religious affiliation was not divisive when I was growing up. Faith in the Creator and goodness to your neighbour was the universal doctrine. Hence, I attended Christian schools for my elementary and high school education: St. Joseph Catholic School, Elegbata Lagos. This gave me a unique opportunity and exposure to both holy books—the Quran and the Bible. These books have parallel teachings and practices.

As part of my discipline growing up, my fierce mother regimented my daily routine. I attended St. Joseph Catholic School for my elementary education, which I started at the age of four. The school was a fair distance from my house, and I walked to and from school every day with the other children in the neighbourhood. We had the morning group and the afternoon group. The morning group was from 8:30 a.m. to noon, and the afternoon group was from 1:00 p.m. to 4:30 p.m.

I preferred the morning school because my routine at home started at 7:00 a.m. anyway. I was expected to wake up early and run errands for my mother, like fetching water carried on my head for household use, then go back and fetch another bucket for bathing. I also helped take my mother's goods to the market (for selling) and would eat and then go to school. Additionally, I preferred the morning school because the temperature was cooler and more tolerable. Nigeria is located north of the Equator, making the climate extremely hot by early afternoon. Therefore, if I were to attend afternoon school, I would have worked for my mother all morning before going to school. Although I still worked after school, it was more physical in nature. After I returned from school, I would change from my school uniform, have lunch, rest a bit, and soon, I was off to sell whatever in-season fruits or products my mother had set on a tray for me. This marked the beginning of my entrepreneurial training, among other life skills. This routine continued for the next five years until I finished elementary school.

With what my young self perceived as a harsh living existence compared to my schoolmates and other children in my neighbourhood, I was determined to not remain close to home for my high school education. In Nigeria, as in most British colonized nations, boarding schools for school-aged children are common, and passing an entrance examination to the parents' chosen schools is mandatory. This was an opportunity for me to escape my daily routine of hard labour, an existence perceived as "child labour" in the Western world.

To facilitate my escape, I failed entrance examinations for schools closer to home in Lagos State. At the same time, I studied diligently to gain admission to schools in other states, even though the boarding fees were additional costs that I knew my parents could not afford after paying the tuition fees. As a child, that reality did not deter me from my plan to escape from home into an unknown world of living away from home at the tender age of twelve. I gained admission to Ebenezer Grammar School, Abeokuta, Ogun State, Nigeria. This marked the first test of my independence and the opportunity to use every bit of training I received from home. I was in boarding school for the next five years with more rigorous daily physical, mental, emotional, psychological, and academic expectations.

The first time I left home for school, my mother sent me off with a very memorable message, reminding me that I was going away to study, to receive an education for a better future and that it was up to me to make better use of that opportunity. Otherwise, I could always return to peddle her goods. I knew she meant every word, and that propelled me to excel academically. It also reminded me to be careful of who I associated with in school. I had to make wise decisions at an early age. School year(s) in and school year(s) out, schoolmates received weekend family visits, but not me. In five years, I received only one unexpected visit from my father. I was delighted! This experience, I believe, also contributed to my independent nature. I only went home during the extended summer breaks as I could not afford to travel far for short school breaks. During the short breaks, I stayed in my hostel with other students in my situation. Those times were pleasant because there was less noise, relaxed rules, and opportunities to leave the confines of the school compound to walk, window shop, and taste local foods in the town markets.

I was a good student in elementary school, especially in English, and received accolades for my penmanship, which was highly valued and recognized in those days. My mother always impressed upon us children that education is a path to a better and more rewarding life.

This aptitude for excellence continued throughout my high school. I occupied my spare time, especially on those visitors' days, when I had no one to visit with me with reading, sports, and different clubs. I was on the literary and debating team and the track and field team. During the regional interhouse sports, I represented my school in the high jump, long jump and javelin. I was also a member of the school's debating team and was the Senior Prefect Girl in my final year of high school. I developed leadership skills and curated my community service skills in that role. I remember always helping the younger students cut their assigned portion of lawn grass during the Friday manual labour under the blazing sun of a tropical country. My penchant for community service and advocacy formed at an early age.

High school was completed, and I returned home in the summer of 1976. It was a bittersweet moment. Over the past five years, all accumulated belongings were gathered with individual and collective memories. Most friendships ended with promises to stay connected through snail letters and photos (there were no phones, cell phones, and no internet). I was happy that I was returning home but sad I was leaving familiarity for uncertainty about the future.

Days turned into weeks and months, and soon, the promise to keep connected dwindled, and the pool of old high school mates shrank while I focused on obtaining employment and putting a plan in place on how to seek admission and fund my post-secondary education. I also decided not to return to my original home in Lagos Island; instead, I chose to reside with my immediate older brother in our family home on the mainland of Lagos. Here, my standard of living improved to a house with running water, a flushed toilet, and a private living space. Although the environment was busy with activities, the neighbourhood was exciting, with offices and street vendors.

By the third month after returning home and no employment, the reality of adulthood began to set in. Yes, I had free accommodation and sometimes free food, too. However, I felt uneasy about not having my own money, which also taught me how to be frugal when I finally got a job as a court clerk with the Lagos State Ministry of Justice.

While I continued to work and saved my money, my brother assisted me with school searches and countries in the West for admissions. The challenge was the fact that no amount of money I saved would be enough for tuition, accommodation, and sustenance. Therefore, the search narrowed to North America, specifically the United States and Canada, countries where I could work and attend school at the same time if I were fortunate enough to obtain a travel permit as a domestic worker.

On January 5, 1978, my travel visa arrived. I resigned from my job, gave away my disposable belongings and used half of my savings to purchase a one-way flight ticket. On February 27, 1978, I flew across the world from Nigeria, West Africa, to Canada. I landed in a foreign land, Calgary, Alberta, leaving behind a hot, tropical climate for an extreme, frigidly cold climate in the heart of Alberta winter. I was one month shy of my twentieth birthday.

So began a new, challenging, lonely, trying, but rewarding and fulfilling life, which I have chronicled in my 2018 published autobiography, I Give *because* I'm Blessed / I'm Blessed *because* I Give: *A Chronicle of An Immigrant's Journey.*

To my children, my three grandchildren (#munchkins), and my future offsprings, I hope this written piece provides a glimpse into my life as a child growing up in a faraway place, a place that you may or may not have an opportunity to experience. However, I do hope that you will try to journey to a place called NIGERIA in West Africa.

ABOUT MOJI TAIWO

Moji Taiwo is the author of I GIVE *because* I'M BLESSED – I'M BLESSED *because* I GIVE: *A Chronicle of An Immigrant's Journey,* available on Amazon worldwide in hardcopy, e-book and Audio downloads. In her book, readers will find "excitement to be their unique self; inspiration to succeed by turning challenges into opportunities; motivation to pursue their dreams and achieve their goals, and strength to challenge the standard norms and the audacity to be Positively Different.

Moji is also the author of *Grandma and Her Munchkins*— An Everyday Adventure Children's picture book series—Books 1 to 5, published in English and French on Amazon and for schools, libraries, and bookstores through IngramSpark.

She's also the creator and host of The Immigrant Experience Show (Tieshow) on her YouTube Channel. Tieshow is intended to be a platform to openly discuss matters of importance to our collective immigrant population (first and second generation), individuals and families. Tieshow highlights who we are as immigrants and our challenges, needs, contributions, aspirations, achievements, and resources. Above all, Tieshow is a promotion and marketing platform.

During her thirty-one years of service with Alberta Justice and Solicitor General, Young Offender Branch, Moji worked tirelessly to improve, impact, and positively shape the lives of young people and their families. She enjoyed training/mentoring young staff and watching them develop and progress in their chosen careers. Equally, she has delivered life skills program classes to youth groups in the community since 1993. She models professionally in her spare time.

Awards: A recipient of many community leadership and professional awards including, but not limited to, the Governor General of Canada, Corrections Exemplary Service Bar Award (2015); the Solicitor General and Public Security Leadership Award (2009), the Corrections Exemplary Service Medal Award (2008) and many other volunteer services awards.

In 2018, Moji Taiwo received the 25th anniversary of the NCAC Volunteer Award and was chosen for the cover story of Lethbridge College's Alumni Magazine 'Wider Horizon.' In 2017, the Canadian Race Relations Foundation featured her story as one of "Canada 150 Stories" (an immigrant success story). In 2022, Moji received the Unmask Your Beauty Black Woman of Influence Award, and in 2023, she received the Queen Elizabeth II Platinum Medal Award from the Government of Alberta. In 2023, she was also honoured with a Lifetime Black Heritage Leadership Award from the Realize Your Potential Youth Society of Canada (RYP).

Moji was a founding and active member of the Nigerian Canadian Association of Calgary (1993), the Yoruba Foundation, Calgary (2004) and founding member/Past President of the Women of Vision Society of Alberta (2012 - 2021).

Moji Taiwo is an avid volunteer for causes that improve the lives of youth, women, families, and her community. Through her board membership at various higher institutions and community organizations, including the Calgary Police Services multicultural unit, she joyfully shares her professional expertise and knowledge as a successful immigrant who is a proud CANADIAN. Most importantly, Moji Taiwo is a wife, mother, and grandmother.

Moji Taiwo – MUT Consulting Services
Creator & Host - Tieshow/Author/Speaker/Coach/
Facilitator/Retired Civil Servant
Website – www.mojitaiwo.com

Always Aim for the Stars in Matters of Love: Know Your Worth and Never Settle for Less

Christine Bode

A stone in my boot is the metaphor for my life. How does it feel to walk with a stone in your boot? Slowly. Awkwardly. Painfully. Putting one foot in front of the other. Searching for that spot where you can take your boot off, shake out the stone, put the boot back on, and keep walking. However, there's another stone in your boot before you know it. And you can do nothing about those stones except learn how to live with them—without anger. Those stones remind you that you're alive and experiencing a human existence. It's over when you can no longer feel the stones in your boots.

Can we learn to be grateful for the stones in our boots? After more than forty years of trying, I'm almost there. And after thirty years of knowing that I should pay attention to the red flags that appear on my path, I finally do. Beware the red flags and proceed with caution. *Develop your intuition and listen to it*; it's the most powerful gift you have for your human experience. And make no mistake, we are spiritual beings having a human experience. I believe it won't be our last, either.

I am a young-spirited sixty-year-old who has never had children. However, I have played a vital role in the lives of my youngest niece and nephew, fraternal twins, who are now twenty-two years old.

Their mother, my middle sister and best friend, Karen, died from ovarian cancer in 2014 at the age of forty-eight when her children were just about to turn twelve. My sister's last words to me were to help her husband with the children because he would need it. I promised her I would. We discovered that women who have had fertility treatments are potentially more at risk for ovarian cancer depending on their age and weight, and my sister Karen had her children later in life, at age thirty-six, after trying for years. She decided to have in vitro fertility treatments because she wanted her children more than anything, and Karen told me that she would make the same decision again, knowing that. Karen's children meant everything to her; now, they mean everything to me. They are my reason for living while I keep emptying stones from my boots and aspiring to be the person they can be proud to emulate or take advice from.

I have always talked to Erika and Ethan as if they were adults. I've always listened to them, asked them questions about their lives and the things they enjoy, and let them know who I really am. An imperfect, diligent, resilient, and generous woman who has never stopped trying to improve myself despite having over fifty jobs, moving over forty times, and weathering the many obstacles that life has put in my path. After being an administrative assistant for over twenty-five years, a self-employed entrepreneur for fifteen years, almost four years of psychotherapy, reading over a thousand books, and making at least a thousand mistakes, I know that life is about the journey and not the destination.

Around the time I was eight years old, I started to put on weight. I'm not sure what triggered my chubbiness, but suddenly, I was larger than the other kids at school, and my mom was putting a lock on the freezer so I couldn't get at the baked goods. By the time I was twelve, I was almost 5' 8" tall and about thirty pounds overweight. So, my mom forced me to go with her to a gym to lose weight, telling me that if I didn't, I would never have a boyfriend in high school. *Those words have stayed with me all my life.* It didn't matter how pretty I was if I was overweight. I wasn't a kid who loved to exercise, except to ride my bike and play outside, go for nature hikes, and walk with our family dog. I was lousy at basketball, which I played when I was young, but I was not graceful or a natural athlete, and I gave it up in high school. In high school and college, I loved to dance and attended many concerts, but I mostly watched a lot of television and movies and frequently resided in the fantasy world I'd created. Sensitive, romantic, and idealistic, I hoped I could someday help make the world a better place with my writing. I also believed in true love, knights on white horses and "someday, my prince will come!"

However, I went to the gym (repeatedly, on and off over the years), which I hated, especially those machines with bands that were supposed to shake your fat away. Ridiculous. I lost weight; when I was thirteen, I looked like I was at least seventeen. After about three months, I weighed 144 lbs and was ready for high school that September.

During the summer of 1977, I went to Calgary to visit my German father's half-brother and his wife, who was from Australia. It was my first trip alone from Kingston, Ontario, where I was born, grew up, and live today, and I trusted my aunt and uncle would take care of me while I was there. However, the first night of my stay, my uncle came into my bedroom, sat on the side of the bed, and although I pretended I was asleep, he started to fondle my breasts. That was as far as it got, but I was terrified, and everything changed for me at that moment. My aunt and uncle were kind but had to work during my visit, so I spent too much time alone in their house, calling my grade school puppy love crush to talk on the phone and ate containers of yogurt and wheels of camembert while they were away (I was about to enter ninth grade and he, eighth. He was gay, became an actor and director, and died at forty-eight from cancer. I kept in touch with him for much of his life). They took me to Banff and Jasper, and I saw the Calgary Stampede Parade, but when I left, I wasn't the same person as when I'd arrived. And I never told anyone about what happened until I was in my thirties and in therapy.

I gained weight during that short trip, and when I entered high school at thirteen, I was too chubby to attract boys, although I was always boy crazy, reading about Shaun Cassidy, Rex Smith, and other teen idols of the day that I fantasized about. I was a photographer and wrote short stories and poetry, too. My first poem, about Shaun Cassidy, was published in Scholastic's *Rock's Biggest Ten*, much to my astonishment. I wrote to pen pals, some female and one male, who became close friends during those years. I had many male friends but no boyfriends, all through high school, despite having a few mad crushes because although I was pretty, more than one teenage boy muttered to me that it was too bad I couldn't lose thirty pounds.

Then, when I was seventeen, I lost my virginity to someone I met at a friend's party in Toronto. *I so wish I hadn't.* I wish I had enough self-respect, self-esteem, self-love, and self-worth not to throw it away. However, I didn't wish on stars back then. Instead, after we stopped seeing each other, I slept with another friend from high school and my best male friend (taking his virginity), becoming quite promiscuous during my late teens, twenties, and early thirties. Then, after having my heart broken for the umpteenth time by the time I was thirty-three, I pretty much gave up on men. I had always hoped that the men I met would want to know the real me and see beyond the pretty face of the overweight woman who was good enough to have sex with but not good enough to commit to. Instead, the first man I lived with was a handsome drug dealer who was on the run from the Hull mafia, and I gave him a place to hide in Toronto in 1987. We broke up in 1989, and I have never lived with another man.

There's no need for me to go on about my failed romantic relationships—and there were many—but the point I want to make is that if I had taken the time when I was young to develop self-respect, self-esteem, self-love, and self-worth, I would not still be single, have trust issues with men, and live without children or grandchildren. However, I learned slowly, despite two college diplomas, through the school of hard knocks, that until we can love ourselves, how can we expect anyone else to love us in return the way we deserve to be loved?

Take the time to lie on your back on the ground as often as possible and look up at the night sky. Feel the grass, breathe deeply, look at the stars and connect with the Universe. It is not malevolent. It does not want our destruction. It is not the reason we struggle as humans. If we look at it long enough, we realize that we are a part of it as it is a part of us. Within us lies the answers to the most challenging questions. We can answer them ourselves if we listen closely enough to the Universe within. If something doesn't feel right to you, it isn't. If it doesn't feel positive, it isn't. It's as simple as that because it's all in our perception of the world.

Life is too short to spend it being miserable, so surround yourself with people who uplift you and challenge you to be the best person you can be. Always treat others the way you want to be treated. Be with people who not only love you but like you for who you are at this very moment. Don't waste your time in romantic relationships with men or women who do not cherish you and treat you with respect, kindness, and admiration. Having things in common is essential, but you don't have to be exactly the same. Opposites do attract and bring something to the relationship that you cannot.

Choose someone you enjoy talking to, who makes you laugh, listens to you, and will hold you when you're grieving. Don't expect them to say or do anything to fix you or the situation. Let them know they don't have to fix you. Don't let someone lie to you more than once; if you let them once, they will do it again. The same goes for cheating. Notice how you feel when you're with them. If you don't feel like a better person who is self-confident and worthy of their love and don't trust them 100 percent, you haven't made the right choice in a partner. If they cheat on you, walk away. If they don't like your dog, walk away. I've had three dogs as an adult who have been like children to me, and they can be enough to keep you company when your family and friends are busy. They are also a significant commitment, and you are responsible for their health and well-being, so always treat them with love and respect.

If a person asks you to change for them, walk away. It doesn't matter if they don't earn heaps of cash. What matters is that they are comfortable in their own skin and treat children, animals and other humans with the same respect, kindness and admiration they treat you with. Walk away if they aren't good to their parents, siblings or children. Because I'm telling you, it's better to be alone than with someone who makes you feel less than good enough just as you are. *You are enough.*

Don't worry about when love will find you. Take the time to work on yourself. Study subjects you're interested in, develop hobbies you're passionate about, work to the best of your abilities, exercise daily, eat as healthily as possible, enjoy your friends, do things for others without expecting anything in return, and read *a lot.* Get off your freaking phones and computers and start talking to people in the real world. You will never meet the person you're looking for if you constantly stay home alone. This I know. Spend as much time as you can with the people in your life who love you and with whom you feel secure. Be with people who want to be with you. Leave the others alone. You don't need them in your tribe. Spend the time that you're not in a romantic relationship, concentrating on enriching the relationships you have with the people you love and who love you. Never settle for being in a romantic relationship that is less than what you deserve.

Self-respect, self-esteem, self-love, and self-worth *are happiness*; until you develop these things, you won't know what it is. Love yourself no matter what size you are. Treat yourself the way you deserve to be treated. We must find happiness within because no one else is responsible for our joy. So, if you're not feeling it now, keep working at it by doing the things that make your spirit shine. Look at the stars—a lot. Get outside daily, walk in nature, and swim or go to a body of water as much as possible. It will ground you and remind you that the Universe is perfect and wants you to be happy. Always aim for the stars in matters of love, and never settle for anyone less than your ideal person. Keep emptying the stones from your boots. You will get what you believe you deserve.

ABOUT CHRISTINE BODE

Christine Bode founded Bodacious Copy, the creative hub where writers' words are sculpted with precision and care. She's the heart and soul behind the scenes, dedicated to elevating your literary works with meticulous copyediting and proofreading prowess. With a passion for polishing outstanding books and a knack for crafting compelling websites, Christine brings a touch of empathy and a wealth of experience to every project.

Her journey with language began at the tender age of fourteen when her poetry first graced the pages of *16 Magazine* and Scholastic's *Rock's Biggest Ten*. A lifelong devotee of literature, she's embraced over 1,000 books with the enthusiasm of a genuine bibliophile. Christine's dedication to reading is matched only by her commitment to ensuring your manuscript captivates its audience.

The accolades for Christine's poetic work, including praise from Sir Bob Geldof and mentorship from broadcasting legend Patrick Watson, have been milestones in her literary adventure. Her published poetry collections, *Eden Refugee* and *Eden Redefined,* have touched hearts, including that of Grammy-winning filmmaker Tom DiCillo.

Beyond poetry, Christine Bode's pen has crafted reviews for esteemed publishers like Simon & Schuster Canada and HarperCollins Canada, and her insights can be found on My Bodacious Blog. Since 2008, she has honed her skills as a freelance copy editor. Since 2012, she has proudly served as the senior copy editor for Publish and Promote, acting as a catalyst for authors' dreams and guiding them to publishing success.

https://bodaciouscopy.com
https://x.com/bodaciouscopy
https://www.linkedin.com/in/christinebode

But What If I Was Wrong?

Sean Robinson

"Isn't it funny how day by day nothing changes, but when you look back, everything is different?"— C.S. Lewis

It shouldn't be a surprise, but we aren't perfect. We are all learning and trying our best; unfortunately, it may not seem like it at times. You may not believe me. I just hope you take my word for it and make fewer mistakes than I did. Then again, this is how we learn and how we grow.

This message will find you when you need it to; it will be exactly what you need at that moment, and until then, you may not believe it. You may think that you are different. That you don't need any help. That you have it all figured out. We were all once the same. We knew everything until we realized we didn't know as much as we thought. Discovering this about ourselves is where growth and appreciation truly begin.

Can you picture the house you grew up in? What was it like? Who was there? Did you like it there? Are you there now? This is a happy memory of a growing family, experiences, and friendships to some. To others, it may not have been the best environment. There may have been negativity, fear, trauma. Wherever you have found yourself, and no matter what has happened with that younger version of yourself, you are here, and you are OK. You are in control of where you go from here, and nothing that has happened can hold you back. I didn't always feel this way, but that is the point. We learn, and we grow. When we know better, we can do better. I know you can do this.

From a young, impressionable child to an older and hopefully wiser adult, significant transitions in life happen to us and for us. Transitions from child to teen to adult, from naïve to cautious to careful, from knowing to learning to understanding. Think about every version of yourself up to this point. There is a good chance that you aren't still living the same life as you did ten years ago, five years ago, last year, this morning. It was such a revelation when I learned that I didn't have to be the same person I used to be. That I could just make different, better decisions. Genuinely thinking that I had become the person I would be for the rest of my life was not far-fetched. I would come to find that this belief is common. Can we simply change? Is it that easy?

There have been many realizations that I have made and five primary truths that I believed about myself in my past life that I had to learn and then correct. This has helped me grow and change the path I was on, both mentally and physically. To become better. I hope you find the message and the example you have been waiting for in these truths and the lessons I learned. It is expected that you will make mistakes similar to and different from mine, but understand that the lessons you learn from this will help you be better; they will help you grow. Correcting these five major beliefs does not define the end of my journey but the foundation I have built to sustain further growth and the creation of the essential pillars that help me continue to grow.

My foundation and growth were held back by the five primary beliefs listed below. Because I thought these were part of my identity, it never occurred to me that I could change them.

1. Excuses made things easy.
2. Reading was not for me.
3. Negativity was a solution.
4. Success was limited.
5. My path was fixed.

Excuses were easy.

Mindset, according to Vocabulary.com, is described as "a habitual or characteristic mental attitude that determines how you will interpret and respond to situations."

When we are focused on being a certain way or have a mindset focused this way, we will do things that lead us closer to what we seek. The easiest way for me to maintain the victim of a fixed mindset was to try and justify the decision that I had made or the "reasons" for not doing something. No matter how we feel about this, they are excuses. An excuse is almost always contextualized negatively. It is a way to justify an action or inaction. I had many that I would use, depending on what was going on. If it was to go for a run or do something outside. It's too hot/cold/dry/damp. It's too early, too late, I'm too tired, or I have too much going on. A reason, as used to explain a situation, may have been accurate and accepted, but I wasn't doing that. I was excusing myself in as many ways to convince those around me—however I needed to—that I couldn't do "the thing," and I left feeling good (shameful) that I dodged another bullet. My excuses were awful, and I started to get lazy with them and "Yeah. Maybe…" was my favourite. I doubt the people around me would expect me to show up or be interested in what was going on, but the maybe I gave was convincing enough that people would leave me alone about it, and I could go on with whatever I felt was more important. The kinds of things I would excuse were often what would make me feel better and help my mental health. But I felt like I was too this and that, and it was more comfortable for me to just say no and continue my life, excusing myself from everything that would benefit me.

Programming our mindset from a place of being fixed is a process, but it is very possible to recover from.

When we start to believe that we can do more, we will be more confident. It is in that confidence that we catch ourselves trying to use one of our favourite excuses again to hide that we plan a better response. If your reason you can't do something is outside of your control, then that is way better than your excuse for not doing it. Catch yourself and your favourite excuses and use a better response. If you can't think of one, get off your backside, do the workout, and read the book or whatever you have been excusing. My best advice is to catch yourself using excuses and write them down. Note a better response beside them so that you can start the programming. Most times, instead of the excuse, just say yes.

Reading was not for me.

For a long time, the people around me weren't talking about reading the latest books or comparing their favourites. In my circles, we would often celebrate not reading for pleasure. It was never something that was forced on me in my childhood. It was something that I could maintain with a bare minimum of effort and mentality. Reading what I had to do for school assignments and day-to-day living without any additional effort was normal and celebrated. I didn't realize how much I was missing in my growth and development and supporting my wellness goals.

Not everyone loves to read, and there will always be a time for television and social media. Still, there is a substantial benefit to disconnecting from the drama and negativity and learning more about a topic or being captivated by a great story. I suspect this will only worsen for future generations, but there is way too much time spent on tablets, phones and other light-emitting devices. There is a lot of science and research behind what this does to your circadian rhythm and sleep quality when time is spent staring at these devices lying in bed before falling asleep. Replacing staring at my phone each night before sleep and reading even only a few pages has compounded how much I have read and how much I've learned. This has also helped my quality of sleep and the many other benefits of proper sleep.

In my own experience, I had no idea what I wanted to do when I finished high school. There is an expectation that at fourteen, fifteen and sixteen years old, we will select the courses that will help us for the rest of our lives. As I approach my fortieth year, I reflect on the period of growth I experienced during this time of my life. I didn't spend a whole lot of time thinking about it. I would figure it out later. Later comes, and hopefully, you have it figured out. Just like in high school, for a long time, I felt the correct information would just show up for me, get inserted into my life, and help me make better decisions. There are a lot of things we learn from what is happening around us, but what if we had better control of this and were able to help ourselves learn more? Reading does this. Having this book and the lessons shared from various perspectives is already going to give you an advantage.

Reading has strengthened my personal development, as I have chosen to focus primarily on nonfiction and self-help. I spent so long believing that I had become the person I would be for the rest of my life and that I had learned everything I would learn. Why wouldn't I think this way? I could go through the days, weeks, months, and years without issues and feel OK. Do we ever challenge the things we are taught or what we learn naturally to be better? To learn more. To do something different than we used to. We can do better when we know better; we can achieve this through constant growth and development. Even if those around you aren't, reading is for everyone and a great way to get closer to the best version of yourself.

Negativity was a solution.

It was easy to be negative about almost every situation. I could justify it however I wanted to, that it would make me believe it was a productive tool in my personal toolkit. I often convinced others that I was a realist who views the world, its problems, and its future and accepts it for what it is. Never with a "fix-it" mentality but more of an "it is what it is" attitude that often had a depressing undertone. There can be benefits to being a realist, but I used it as an excuse to be cynical and find the negative in almost every situation. This negativity was never helpful and only drove me into an acute depression and those around me further away.

Think about your life and the people you have had for reasons, seasons and lifetimes. Did you know anyone who was always pessimistic and cynical? Did you enjoy their company and want to spend more time with them, or did you count down the minutes until the experience was over? I expect that it was the latter. People who find the worst in every situation, even if it is somewhat accurate, never make a moment better. They just bring the rest of the group and general attitude down. I was this person, and just as I gradually found myself with that attitude and mentality, I gradually pulled myself out of it.

I think, like most personal traits, we may like to change; we focus on the mountain that is in front of us and how difficult it will be to be different, to be better rather than how we can simply work on it. With much judgment, I would roll my eyes and "throw stones" at overly optimistic and happy people. It didn't seem real. What kind of drugs were they on?

Being more positive and programming ourselves away from the negativity we may be around is all about perspective. It is about how we analyze the moment and react to it. It is about appreciation of this life, empathy and understanding for ourselves and those around us and knowing what we can and can't control. For instance, it is easy to be upset and find the bad on a dark, gloomy, rainy day. Maybe we had hoped to be outside all day, playing in the sunshine, but plans have changed. It doesn't take much effort to start thinking about this differently. Now that it is raining, I get to spend more time reading my book, playing board games with my kids, watching a movie I want to watch, visiting, and having coffee with a friend. The sunshine will come, and we can do the other things another time.

Programming, as it relates to our negativity and cynicism, is crucial to start appreciating what we have and making the best of it. Thinking about a moment and how it could be positive is the main thing that I had to realize. The other thing was how I compared myself to other people. I would see someone with a level of success or growth and feel that it should be something I should have, or why not me? Comparing to others is something we should try to avoid. We are all on different paths and at various levels. We will all arrive at every moment at a different time than others and when we're ready. Just keep going, and your time will come.

Success was limited.

There is plenty of success around us in the news, on social media, and at local events. We see people achieving all the most amazing things. For so long, I felt that there was some sort of cap on the amount and level of success that could be achieved. Like the limit was out there, and if someone I knew had a level of success, that meant the cap was reached, and there wasn't enough for me, too. This would also result in negativity and cynicism towards my potential and the success of others, as mentioned above.

There are many positive points to take from this that I hope you may start to believe. When it comes to success and abundance, there is no cap, and anyone can achieve it. We just have to look at it differently. To start, we are all different and will excel at different things. You may not make the professional sports team like someone in your town or create the most incredible new phone app like that person on Facebook, but what are you good at? What can you create? How much work are you putting into being better at the things that mean something to you? Success is earned and comes to those who put in the most work towards it. Trust me, even if it seems like something is handed to someone or they became "an overnight success," nobody sees the substantial amount of work in the background that has led them to this point.

Malcolm Gladwell's book *Outliers: The Story of Success* and Anders Ericsson and Robert Pool's book *Peak: Secrets from the New Science of Expertise* discuss the 10,000-hour rule and deliberate practice. Essentially, the amount of work and effort put into something, and the constant improvement will eventually lead to you becoming great at it. You really can do anything you want to do and be successful at it, but are you putting in enough work?

There is no success you can't achieve and no cap on the amount of people that have it. Just keep putting in the reps, and great things will come.

My path was fixed.

The theme of personal growth and development is woven like a web. All areas will meet at some point, and the strategies can be translated into the different areas. Like my focus above, there are a lot of similarities in the beliefs that I maintained. All were held in my mind and at my own discredit. Regarding our potential and path, it is easy to feel we are on a fixed path with a predetermined destination. To look at where we are born, where we live, what our parents or family did or where we went to school, it is easy to feel like we might be stuck in a situation. It is easier for some people, and as mentioned, comparison is the worst thing we can do.

I always felt my path was fixed. Like I could only be a handful of things. Why did I think this way? There was so much success around me. Generationally, there was an expectation that you had to go to university, live in a specific area and have generational wealth to change your path or live a different life. This may have made this easier, but I had to believe I could be anything I wanted, regardless of my background. And we can.

Your path is where you are headed. And if something comes up, and it will, the direction may change. The change may be because you learned more, changed your mind, found something better or simply just couldn't complete the things required to get there. This is normal, and our paths are never fixed. We just need to keep moving. You determine the path you want to take and must do the work to get there. This has nothing to do with anyone else or anything else. You have control. Once I realized this, I could get behind the things and the mentality I needed to get through some more challenging times and some areas I had no experience in.

Conclusion

It may seem difficult and take a while, but you can change at any moment. You can start to live the life you have always wanted. The things that I believed and carried with me as my truths were never going to help me grow and be better. They were only going to hold me down and prevent any growth. It wasn't until I started to learn and be open to the potential that I was wrong that I found the strength and confidence to create a new story for myself. This wouldn't come on its own, and there wouldn't be any special delivery from outside my creation. This doesn't mean that I had to do it by myself. I needed my family, friends and the people in my life to help me feel encouraged and supported to change. I was wrong in all the primary beliefs that I carried. Excuses seemed easy but made my life very difficult. I let others influence me to avoid reading and have found substantial growth in the things I have learned from reading. Positivity will make every situation easier, and finding the negative will only make it worse. There is unlimited success for anyone who seeks it, and my path was never fixed.

I challenged my beliefs and what I thought was true. What do you believe?

ABOUT SEAN ROBINSON

Sean Robinson became an author and speaker in 2022 with the birth of his first book, *Going Dry: My Path to Overcoming Habitual Drinking.*

Sean is also a mindset coach who focuses on self-improvement, mindset shifting, and changing habits. He works with groups and individuals, coaching them to create healthy habits, live healthier lives, and challenge old mindsets.

Sean Robinson also works as a manager in the construction industry and is a volunteer firefighter. He lives with his wife and three children in Ontario, Canada.

Learn more at https://seanrobinson.ca.

Black Frames

Sharon Kamassah

The core of me is BLACK. My identity. My definition of self. It is all framed in Black.

My vision is all hues, tones, heat, and cools of Black. For me, Black could never be lacking or static. In fact, I remember feeling enraged the first time I heard Black defined as the absence of colour and light. We all ought to know that when you spend time with Black, look deeper and give it space; Black is *limitless.* A Spirit. A rhythm. A connection. All colours brought together in one.

My walls are filled with black frames. Every height. Every width. Wood matte and glossy hard plastics. Textured and smooth. Frames that hold snippets of my life to remind me of who I am and where I've been.

Every morning, when I open my eyes, there they are to greet me. These frames remind me that I am part of something bigger. I may be in different seasons, but the core of me never changes.

The frames were an exhale that helped ground me when I found myself floating. Their presence multiplied after my mother transitioned, a season that left me feeling untethered and wondering. In her absence, my steps forward felt like walking on shifting sand. The black frames, though, gave me something to grasp onto and a feeling of stability.

Questions whirled within me in the wake of her departure, prompting me to capture possibilities in the irregular black squares.

Who was I in my mom's eyes before she took her last exhale?

Who am I when I finally decide to exhale myself?

Uncovering Pieces

Born of a woman who hoarded everything from receipts to feelings, I will never know all she tucked away inside. Looking for clues, I spent two years excavating after my mother passed away. I fondly call them my rest and purging years, though I know I need to do both perpetually. I meticulously sifted through stacks of scrap papers with random numbers scrawled on them. Creased, browned photos of people I don't recognize. Dusty sheaths of decadent velvet and intricately beaded fabrics at the bottom of plastic tubs. A library full of notebooks, bills, magazines, newspaper clippings, birthday cards, funeral announcements, and more.

I was torn. I was excited to discover unknown parts of my mother and sad that even though she left all this behind, I still needed her to decipher it for me. If I could go back in time before the stroke stole her away from me, I would ask her what she was hiding underneath all that stuff she collected. What did she think would happen if she lowered the façade of hyper-self-protection and just allowed herself to be known? Vulnerable? Taken care of? These questions sat with me so heavily that I was in danger of continuing her and her mother's tradition of keeping every scrap my hands laid on. Holding tightly to Mom's stuff as proof that she was once here.

The more I've uncovered, the more resolute I've become to give my children keys to our inner worlds. Gradually, I uncover fragments of her and me, each revelation incrementally freeing me. I embrace these pieces. Mindfully, I frame these breakthroughs in Blackness for all to see. The rest I release.

Embracing Pieces

Sometimes, when I glance in the mirror, I see her looking back at me. Lately, I've warmed to her visitations. She grins when I adorn myself with odd fabrics that only singer Prince would don in public. Well, Prince and my mother. For instance, I recently found one of her hats and immediately flashback to my wedding in Ghana. It was a sparkly white sequin cap, which she paired at the time with a lightly feathered dress. There, in the Motherland, was my mother, sitting in the front row, proud and regal. She glowed, and I remember thinking about how joy-filled and beautiful she looked at the time. Didn't matter that she'd never been on African soil.

Didn't matter that everyone else wore multi-patterned African cloth and hand-painted beads. She sat tall. I don't even think it dawned on her that she stood out. Her demeanour screamed she was home.

Strangers would be surprised that before her disease, my relationship with my mother was not smooth sailing. We frequently clashed, being different sides of the same coin. Now that she is gone, I wish I had more compassion towards her. I now recognize she navigated life's challenges essentially alone. I reflect on how she was raised in Jamaica, an only child reared by a single father into her late teens. Almost by premonition, her father succumbed to his second stroke and died by the time she was in her early thirties. Soon after, she was raising two daughters alone in a country without much family or true friends around. She lacked a sturdy village to support her, so she worked around the clock for most of her adult life, staunchly independent, making strides as she saw fit. I believe having an entity she could lean on was profoundly crucial for her, so she delved deeply into her Christian faith later in life. God was a constant she could turn to even if she or others were disappointed, which is something I never truly appreciated when she was with me. Like her, I was always independent-minded (or stubborn, as she often called me). However, I travelled and took risks simply because I found community and did things she openly thought were nonsensical, incomprehensible, and outright hated. This meant we locked horns more frequently than I care to remember.

But she was always Mom. She was Grandma. She was ours.

Until she wasn't.

Framing New Beginnings

After years of her just existing, I expected to feel peace when her body finally drew its last breath. Instead, I went into shock. It dawned on me that I ran out of time. When her eyes clouded over, my first instinct was to shift into do mode. *I have to make funeral arrangements. Who is going to take her to the parlour? I have twenty-four hours to clear the room. Who can I call?* When feelings started to creep in, I chided myself. *She is now in a better place. Her spirit is free. She's no longer moored to a useless body. She is not in pain. Get it together!* I floated for months after her "celebration of life," trying not to feel anything. In reality, though, I felt heavy with grief.

Purging became a means of coping, a process of releasing the unresolved weight of decades. I sifted and let go of her and my papers that I had carried with me from house to house since the Eighties. I cringed as I read old diaries and tossed them into overflowing banker boxes to burn along with ancient love letters, invoices and work plans.

Then I found her card. I found a whisper of her voice.

This undated birthday card currently hangs framed prominently on my wall. The first time I read it, I thought it would fill me with sadness, but instead, it served as a testament to her very essence. This card was so my mother. Her penmanship was artful, razor-straight, and precise. My mother rarely said "I love you" directly when she could, and this letter was no different. Still, I felt her care. It started with *Your birthday falls at a very special time of the year for the Christian world and especially to me, and no matter what, that makes you very special to me.* By the end, she admitted: *I'm still learning—the Holy Spirit is my Teacher—and my prayer is that the Holy Spirit will give you the understanding and enable you to walk this love walk, and then we can say and agree that truly you have become a success.*

Happy Birthday – God's special girl.

Imperfectly perfect, I gently hung it by my bedroom door. I've read it almost every day since, and slowly, these truths have settled in me with every reading.

I will never fully know my mother. And that is alright.

I know enough.

I am grateful she was here and gave me as much as she did, to the best of her ability and insight.

She was enough and will always be enough.

My next season, beginning with this chapter, is to be shamelessly known.

Perfectly imperfect.

Knowing I also am enough.

This is part of what it means to walk this love walk. To unconditionally love who I came from, who I am, and what I am for those who come after me. To love those I have the privilege to walk this earth with. That's it.

The card also is a reminder that she is still with me. Her reminder is that no matter how things may appear, I will never walk this life alone, for spirit is eternal.

We will always be a piece of one another, framed in Black.

ABOUT SHARON KAMASSAH

Sharon Kamassah, PhD, is a social worker, educator, and consultant. She was raised by Jamaican parents in Toronto, Canada, where she continues to thrive. Writing is not a choice for her. Stories fill her every day, compelling her to write them joyfully. She loves to rescue books from every secondhand shop, and almost every wall of her home is lined with volumes to prove it. The mother of three enjoys frequent trips with her family, driving along highways with the beats blaring. She dedicates this piece to the much-loved grandmother of her children, who was the very embodiment of resilience and audacity. Her spirit lives on!

A War Orphan's Story: Make the Best of Where You Land

Klaus Armstrong-Braun

My tale is the account of a Polish boy orphaned at four, journeying through loss, loneliness, fear, uncertainty, love and hope in war-torn Germany, post-war rural Ireland, and eventually adult life in England.

On September 1, 1939, without a formal declaration of war, Nazi Germany invaded Poland. The Soviet troops invaded Poland on September 17, 1939. A German soldier from Essen named Braun met my mother, Luiza, in Krakow. He fell in love with her, but nobody knew if they were married.

I, Klaus Braun, was born on December 13, 1940, a Kriegskinder (war child). I had no birth certificate and never knew my father, who went off to fight the Russians and probably was killed at the Battle of Stalingrad.

It was not a good time or place to come into the world!

Meine Mutter (My Mother)

My mother, Luiza, became homeless and put me in an orphanage at three and a half years of age in April 1944, at the Goldschmidt Kinderheim (Children's Home) in the Schulenbergwald. She sometimes visited me.

On her first visit, she came to collect me. At first, I did not know her, but as we walked downhill to Bredenscheid railway station, I began to feel close to Mutter, holding her hand continuously. We climbed into a railway coach, where we would sleep for the night. I snuggled up close to her, feeling loved and safe—a feeling I have rarely had—and dozed off. I woke, startled as the coach was shunted. "Go back to sleep, my darling." She crooned a lullaby with me lying on her lap, "Sleep, little one, sleep, outside are the sheep, black and white." In the morning, we left early and walked back to the orphanage.

On her last visit, she took me out, but bombing started, so we walked back. I was horrified to see many dead bodies and bits of bodies. *War is horrible.* That was the last I saw of her; soon afterwards, she was killed when the station was bombed. I had become a war orphan. Those memories of Mutter are precious because I never again felt a mother's love.

CONFLICT

strife

unrest

uprisings

terror

wars

RESULT

fleeing

refugees

death

FLOTSAM

A piece of flotsam on a lonely shoreline?

A wee baby.
Nameless.
Where from?
Looking up with glazed eyes,
a streak of terror emblazoned in its tiny eyes.
Little hands clenched,
clutching for a mother not there.

Goldschmidt Haus

Goldschmidt Haus was set in a forest, away from the Allied bombing of towns, run by nurses, with about eighty-eight children. We often walked into the forest and played.

I remember being in an area of grass so tall that I had to jump up and down to see ahead. I aimed for the house. Fatigued with jumping up and down, I panicked, shouting loudly when I jumped up. After a time, a lady appeared coming towards me. She held my hand and, in a non-frightening voice, led me to steps with a door at the top. We climbed up and came into a massive room with a multitude of objects. This was the kitchen.

Aunty Elist, the Superintendent, was a very kind lady filled with love. As my guardian, she kept in contact with me after I reached Ireland. I got on well with her even though I was naughty. I was learning to feel safe with people. Unfortunately, these friendly nurses were replaced by nasty "Hitler Nurses," and beatings became common.

Evacuation From Essen, Germany to Glencree, Ireland (1945)

Toward the end of the war, millions of civilians were homeless or starving from Allied bombing. Many parents, no longer able to care for their children, sent them abroad for safety.

Dr. Kathleen Murphy established the Save the German Children Society in Dublin to save "as many German children as possible from death by starvation." More than 280 Irish families offered to foster German children, and we orphanage children were evacuated to Glencree, Ireland. This was the forerunner of Operation Shamrock.

One day in October 1945, the morning dawned, and German Red Cross lorries came into the Goldschmidt grounds to pick us up, each of us taking only a small bag of essential clothes. Being packed into the lorries to start a week-long journey was exciting. As the lorries departed, I looked back at our "family home" with sadness.

The lorries drove for a day until we came to a big house to spend the night, then onwards to a railway station, where we excitedly boarded rail coaches. Two days by train brought us to what looked to me like a big, strange-looking "house," into which we were hustled. Soon, the "house" (a ship) was floating on a large expanse of water, eventually coming to a port, Dun Laoghaire, Dublin, Ireland. We were offloaded into lorries to end up at Glencree Irish Red Cross Reception Centre.

I was bewildered. What was happening to us?

Driftwood

I was taken in by a host family, but they could not cope with a troubled boy who spoke only German. I went to another, then another, and was placed with fourteen host families over ten years—Bray, Carrigan, Dublin, Belfast, Leitrim, Killeshandra, Kildanan, Kildare, and Fontstown. One woman's husband had died from wartime wounds while fighting in Germany, and she seemed to take revenge on me for being German, treating me like a servant. At another place, the host tried to kill me in a rage. It was very unsettling. I was a "Pass the Parcel kid," like a piece of driftwood.

Driftwood

Here I go, there I go
A drifter floating where life bade me to.
Where will I be tomorrow night?

In a ship's hull, I lived, travelling the seas
With other planks playing my part,
Keeping those seas from coming inside.

But life is real; life is luck.
A landing stage did pluck me out.
Why me?

Before, I was a tree so young.
But down I came whilst others stayed,
A useless life ahead of me.

On a beach, I landed, hope at last; peace!
But not for me, that drifting wood,
There lurks a beachcomber ready to pounce.

A fire awaits me to keep him warm
With other poor driftwood to share my fate.
Another change in fortune, so.

My earthly form has lost its shape.
As a driftwood spirit, I have become
Aimlessly drifting in the seas of time.

© Klaus Armstrong-Braun

My Sweet Love, Adelade

One evening, a lovely girl, Adelade, came with her mother and brother to visit my host in Fontstown. "Children must be seen and not heard" was the rule then. All I could do was just sit, looking at her. Adelade was slim, a bit taller than me, with long black hair and a sharp-featured face, wearing a black dress. Her brute brother glowered at me all evening. As she left, I felt forlorn.

However, I gave her a special salutation, and a few days later, I spotted her walking towards me down a sunken track with trees and bushes overhead. I was overjoyed. Earlier, I had built a platform in a tree and invited her up to sit beside me. We talked for a long time until she said, "I'd better go back, or my brother will give us trouble." We climbed down, and I gave her a peck.

But the next time I saw her, she was different. She told me she could not see me again because:

I was Protestant, and she was Catholic,

I was German and

I had no family nor fixed abode.

Down the track came her brother, shouting to take her away. I quickly gave her a last kiss, and we were parted. To this day, I still think of her. The platform was still there when I returned fifty years later!

After that, I lost another girl for the same reasons. I never married. With no mother and no wife, I have felt lonesome all my life. Oh, the driftwood curse…it also affected me at schools and colleges. But I have not let it defeat me and have filled my life with many good things.

Daddy Armstrong (Cavan, Carrigan, Ireland)

At one home, however, I found real love. Robert Armstrong was a "converted" Christian, and he talked to me about God and His creation (nature) and always spoke about the Bible. It was a profound discourse that was very inspiring for a young boy. It made me what I am today.

For example, one day, I ran across a patch of daffodils, and he told me off, "Those are God's creatures. You shouldn't harm God's creatures; you should be good to other people and help everybody." I have remembered that ever since.

I called him "Daddy" because he loved me so much, and I loved him. When I was baptized in Kildallon Church, "Daddy Armstrong" gave me his surname, which I later added to mine by deed poll so his name would not be forgotten. I became Klaus Armstrong-Braun.

Daddy Armstrong and his wife, Fanny's two daughters, came home from Sligo Boarding School for the holidays. The first thing they said when they came was, "You smell!" Out came the tin bath and a scrubbing brush, and I was tortured.

One day, Daddy Armstrong told me, "You have a little brother, Willi. He is coming to live with us." I was horrified, not knowing I had a brother, and did not want one. Was it because I didn't want to share their love with anyone? In my drifting around, Willi was sometimes with me, sometimes not, and eventually, we lost touch.

Daddy Armstrong had been a prisoner of war. As the doctors were useless, he became ill from stomach ulcers.

His wife, Fanny, was sick and deaf. After a year, Daddy and Fanny became worried that if he had a problem or she died, nobody could look after me, so he tried to find me a better place, and my drifting began again.

Schools

In Ireland, I went to several schools. At school in Cornacrum, Carrigan, I wrote with the usual ink pen, but one day, a toffee-nosed kid came in with a biro (ballpoint pen). We all gawped jealously. I got Daddy A to buy me one. When the ink stopped flowing, I unscrewed the barrel and found a tube inside, open at the top, so I filled it with my ink pen and waited to see what would happen. Behold, it worked! It was not long before the makers squeezed the top to prevent self-filling. So, I un-squeezed the top and continued self-filling the biro. I was a budding engineer!

At school in Athy, Kildare, one chum had loads of comics and annuals, mostly of cowboys, American Indians and robbers. He would invite us in to read them and sometimes lend me some. I was transported into these comics and wanted to live as a cowboy, which helped me escape the cruelty of my then-hosts.

However, one day, I realized I could not live in those comics because I would have to grow up. I was horrified because I found most adults horrible. I loved the bogs and trees around me but realized I would have to leave them. It depressed me, and I wanted my life to end. I asked God if I could stay as I was, and He answered in His way, giving me the thought that in the Bible, it was a sin to commit suicide. I would have to carry on with life, accepting my future as a man as it would be. This thought helped me later in life.

To England

At age fourteen, I went to live at Dr. Barnardo's children's home in Boughton Hall, Chester. I liked living there because it was like a big family. Joining the Boys Brigade, I loved playing the bugle. In several Irish schools, they said I was good at engineering. At school in Chester, I loved metalwork, always doing more than the teachers required of me.

Engineering was in my soul; was it because of my German roots? At the age of sixteen, I went to Chester College of Further Education, then Byron Street College of Technology, Birkenhead, obtaining certificates and qualifications to meet the engineering criteria in Production and Mechanical Engineering, which I studied at John Moore's University, Liverpool. I was now a member of the UK Association of Professional Engineers. Not bad for a scallywag, driftwood orphan with an unsettled upbringing!

Sport

My first attempt at sport was a sack race at Cornacrum School. The sack was taller than I was, and I came last. Then people told me, "You are for the high jump." Did that mean I was in trouble? No, it was the actual high jump. I was too short—but inventive. Noticing a slope on one side of the jump, I ascended it to gain height and flew over the bar! I got a medal! A future star or an abysmal nonstarter?

When I got to Chester, I enjoyed badminton. To be fit for matches, I would run two miles beforehand. I liked running, which eventually became my primary sport, and I won many races, long and short. I became very good at it, partly because I didn't need to drink much during races. For example, I took part in the Western (United) States Endurance Run for twenty-four hours across the Sierra Nevada Mountains' old pioneer trail, in which we covered 100 miles and endured 18,000 feet of climbing. I won the Gloucester twenty-four-hour track race, running 125 3/4 miles.

Sports kept my mind off loneliness and boredom and could be the reason for remaining healthy even at the age of eighty-plus.

Community and the Arts

Throughout my life, I have written short stories, poems, songs, and music, some of which have been performed at public concerts. Some came from my dreams, some from life. Now, late in life, I am writing my memoir, *War and Its Orphan: A Lost Child*, which I hope to share with the world soon.

I took up several forms of dancing and have acted in several plays, but my primary art form is singing, which I love. I started singing at Goldschmidt when I was three and a half years old and then in church services and school classes in Ireland. In Fontstown Church, the organist recognized several children who could sing in tune, including me, and formed us into a new choir. I still sing with various choirs, sometimes solo.

If you like writing, acting or singing, keep doing what you love! You never know who else may enjoy your creative gifts.

Working Life

I became an apprentice fitter at Chester Hydraulic Engineering Company, training for engine maintenance of ships. Then I moved to the railways, first at the Locomotive Depot in Chester, then North Wales, and in Stoke as a "Cripple Wagon" Inspector, and finally became a Wagon Maintenance Supervisor at British Rail Wagon Shop in Chester.

Tragically, in 1985, an accident crippled me, kyboshing my engineering future and my sports. I was trying to lift heavy brake gear, using even my neck, but the strain was too much, and I fractured vertebrae and ligaments, which I still suffer from today. Though I had operations,

I could not continue working and was pensioned off and unemployed for the rest of my life.

But this gave me much free time, and I decided to use it well.

Community Service and Becoming an Environmentalist

Since my accident retired me young, I have used my time in community work, especially in environmental matters and campaigns. I also do voluntary advocacy.

Instead of a paid career in engineering, I switched to an unpaid career in environmental action, obtaining an Honours Environmental Science Degree at Manchester Metropolitan University and a post-graduate degree in biology at Chester University.

Becoming an environmentalist requires a love for the natural world and a single-mindedness to persist against the odds. The seeds of both were sown early on in my life at Goldschmidt Haus, surrounded by forest, and were added to and watered in Ireland, where I was surrounded by countryside, hills, and mountains. Since in most places I stayed, there were few humans to talk to, I would speak to the plants, animals, and birds around me and pretend they could talk to me. If anyone hurt them, I would get upset.

I watched how Daddy Armstrong lived out his Christian faith and how he farmed his land with consideration for his animals, wildlife and even the wild plants. In any activity he carried out, he wanted to minimize harm to them because everything was God's creation, and he was given them to look after. If he did, they would provide for our needs as well.

Environmental Battles

My first environmental battle was when I was about seven years old.

One Sunday, the sermon was about not killing God's creatures just for fun, but coming into the rectory land from church, I found a hare hunt happening. I saw the hare being torn apart and was horrified. I told Reverend Jennings off for allowing it.

In 1949, there was a drought. While walking to Carrigan-on-Shannon School on a boiling hot day, I saw, in a field, grown cattle and calves suffering without water to drink. The next day, the same problem occurred. I mentioned this to Mr. Anderson, Headmaster, who helped me make a complaint to the Junior Society for Prevention of Cruelty to Animals. The farmer got told off and installed a water trough in the field. Not bad for an eight-year-old.

Lessons of a Troublemaker

I learned to become a troublemaker where and when it is required. Becoming involved with Dr. Andrew Basden in campaigning for the Green Party, I worked with him to submit comments on environmental plans at various levels (local, district, county). That meant attending Local Plan enquiries for weeks on end to fight bad environmental policies, which would also often impact humans. I progressed to national and even international levels (UK, Greece, Romania, Ireland, Gibraltar, the EU and the European Court of Justice), where I got laws changed. People at various levels of government learned to think appropriately about the environment.

I was learning from experience how to work effectively in courts and with the Environmental Law Foundation.

The Way Forward for You

As I approach the end of my life's sojourn, born at the beginning of a devastating World War, a lonesome orphan traversing through four countries like a piece of driftwood, landing in many varied situations and having to adjust, I can see that my hard life gave me the resilience to take the twists and turns of later life, the courage and engineering ability to act and to constantly learn deep love for the natural world, with the faith that God helps me.

I am grateful to have landed on one occasion with one person who gave me strength, love, guidance and happiness: Daddy Armstrong. I hope I have done him proud.

Seven principles I live by and recommend:

1. Put your trust in the Lord at all times. Motto: God first, Man second, Self last.
2. Manners Maketh Man. Always say "Please."
3. Fight for justice at all times.
4. Never let anyone down. Be trustworthy and reliable so others have faith in you.
5. Cherish the Earth because it's the only home we have, and our grandchildren will need it.
6. If you feel you have something to give, don't wait to be asked; always offer yourself, or if need be, take action.
7. Lastly, *never give up*. Wherever the driftwood lands, make the best of it.

ABOUT KLAUS ARMSTRONG-BRAUN

Klaus, now eighty-four, lives in Broughton, Chester, England. He was born in Nazi-occupied Poland in 1940, with the Second World War raging around him. As an orphan of war, Klaus was shipped off to neutral Ireland as a refugee.

He moved from host family to host family—fourteen times in ten years, ending up in Chester, where he worked as an engineer.

Klaus believes his early experience shaped his environmental and political outlook, and he has served on many local councils (Mayor of Saltney, Flintshire County Councillor, and currently Broughton & Bretton Community Councillor) and with national bodies to ensure they conserve our planet's most vulnerable species and ecosystems and help local people.

Setting Yourself Up for Social and Financial Success

Caroline Barrow

Growing up with Caribbean parents of Guyanese heritage, my parents always used to say, "There's no such thing as a free lunch." This simple sentence can be translated into many different forms. Think about it: when you go out for lunch, and if you are invited out to lunch by someone who will pay for your lunch, it's free, right? Well, it's not exactly free—you may end up leaving a tip, or you may have driven to lunch, so it cost you gas, or you may have taken an Uber and paid for it. You may have had to pay for parking too, or if you didn't have to do any of that, then the cost was time. As you navigate this thing called life, you will realize that time is money, time is valuable, time can be used to think of ways to make money and so on. Time is certainly precious and should be used wisely every single day. More on time later in the chapter, so let's focus on the money part for now.

So, back to the "free lunch." You also gain from the free lunch through conversation, networking opportunities, or advice, so although it may cost you time, it could also mean time well spent. You may have heard people say you can't have money and time. Either you have lots of money but no time as you are always working, *or* you have lots of time and no money because you are never working, or in extreme circumstances, some of the lucky ones inherit money or win the lottery. For the sake of this chapter, no one won the lottery, and no inheritance was involved. What would you rather, time or money? If you get the right balance, both can be very rewarding. Will that bring ultimate happiness to your life? Maybe. Will having money make you happy? Perhaps. By money, I mean disposable income. What is disposable income?

Simply put, it is money after mandatory charges and expenses are paid and is available to be spent or saved as you wish. Have you ever heard people say money does not buy you happiness? Yes, that is undoubtedly true. Believe it every time you hear it. However, money can buy you opportunities and experiences and put you in a place to succeed, leading to happiness.

When I was at school, financial wellness was not one of the core subjects. I still don't understand why it is not a core subject in school nowadays, unlike algebra. In the real world, you do not use algebra, but you absolutely need financial awareness. Starting in middle school, I think they should teach financial awareness and then, in high school, about investments (short and long-term), assets like property investments, property management, mortgages, taxes, etc. It will help students understand the cost of a home and what it takes to maintain a home. Just buying a home is not enough. If you are not smart about your home purchase, it could end up costing you in the long run. The upkeep of a home and the property is also essential. This can affect your home's equity and lower the property's value.

Equity is the market value of your property, so in order to get the best-appraised value for your home, you have to take care of it to the best of your ability. This includes outside the house, your front yard, your back yard and everything in between.

There is always something to do in your home, and students/young people, if you have your own room, that is a blessing. Not many people grew up having their own room. Some of us had to share bedrooms with siblings. Growing up, I had to share my bedroom with two of my sisters, which meant that I could not play my music in the comfort of my room, and I couldn't always bring my friends to play with dolls in our own space as it was always occupied. No privacy. I couldn't play cassette tapes on my boom box system without disturbing one of my sisters. In those days, TVs were not allowed in bedrooms. We only had one TV in the family room. These days, students have TVs, game consoles, wireless speakers, walk-in closets, and sitting areas, all in their own bedrooms; none of these things should be taken for granted. They are all blessings.

Homeownership could change your trajectory and the outcome of your life for you and your future family. There are many steps to achieving homeownership, but it all starts with knowledge. As a licensed Realtor, I have consulted with many people in their thirties, forties and fifties who would love to own a home of their own one day. Here are five key factors you must do in this process as a youngster to set yourself up for social and financial success. And I'm talking to you, the grandchildren, about what you must do now in the market:

1. As soon as you turn eighteen, open a bank account. Your parents may have an account for you in their name or an account for you linked to theirs; however, you need your own account separate from your parents. Therefore, at eighteen, get your own bank account. Ensure it is at a regular bank that you can access easily and where you can go in and talk to a human being. Internet bank accounts are OK, too, but it is best to have a brick-and-mortar location where you can speak to a banker. In addition to a traditional bank, open a checking or savings account with a credit union. The most significant differences between the two establishments are as follows:
    - Banks are typically for-profit institutions and are focused on making money. Very helpful and useful, especially if you are interested in doing business overseas or travelling overseas; your money will be easily accessible.

- Credit Unions are for members only and are non-profit institutions. They are generally smaller than banks, operate regionally and may have low interest rates on car loans and higher interest rates for savings and investments.

2. The next smart financial move will be to open a Roth IRA account and start with a five-dollar investment. If you can put in five dollars weekly for five years straight without touching it, you will be on a great start to building your retirement fund. Yes, I know it sounds crazy to even put the word retirement out there in a book for grandchildren, but if more of us had started putting away money earlier from a young age, it would have paid off in our thirties, forties and fifties. Roth IRAs are special Individual Retirement Accounts in which you pay taxes on your contributions (the money you invest), but all withdrawals are tax-free. It's long-term savings, so investing five dollars (minimum) in the account weekly until you're ready to buy your first home is a great way to save for the downpayment. When you are ready to withdraw the funds for the deposit for your home purchase, you won't pay any tax on that money.

3. Building credit and maintaining good credit is one of the most important things you must do starting at a young age. This leads to your FICO score, more commonly known as your credit score.

   FICO is an acronym for the Fair Issac Corporation. FICO developed a three-digit number, the score, which helps lenders determine how likely you are to repay a loan. This, in turn, affects how much you can borrow, how many months you have to repay and how much it will cost (the interest rate). When you apply for a credit card, lenders will use the FICO score to make quick decisions within seconds whether or not you are credit worthy. Therefore, do not apply for loans or credit cards multiple times, as the number of inquiries will affect your score. In other words, it can affect everything financially that will eventually matter to you and mean so much, like a car, a home/mortgage, a loan for large purchases or a business line of credit.

Living in the Western world, your creditworthiness is a major part of your well-being. A bad credit score can cost you more in the long run for the same things a good or excellent credit score will cost you. Don't get me wrong, although you can recover and get yourself out of a low credit rating, protecting it in the first instance should always be your goal and will make you more successful earlier in your adult life. Some companies check your credit score before offering you a job, depending on the industry you are applying to for that opportunity. For example, the financial sector or any industry related to finance and integrity will run your credit report as part of your background check. Here are the different scores and their meaning:

- Excellent – 800+: Very likely to get the lowest rates on loans and be approved.
- Great – 740 – 799: Likely to get low loan rates and be approved.
- Good – 670 – 739: Rates will vary depending on your total outstanding debt (if any) but will likely get approved at good rates (may not be the lowest).
- Fair – 580 – 669: Loans will be expensive and cost you in the long run. Get your score above 670.

- Poor – 300 – 579: Not creditworthy. Get your score above 670.

Make it a habit to protect your credit score throughout your life. Do not ever open a credit card in your name on behalf of someone else or for someone else to use. If that someone does not adhere to the rules of the credit card company, it could be detrimental to your credit score. If you choose to help someone with credit, like a spouse, then make them an authorized user on your account instead, and if they don't follow the rules, then you can remove them from your credit card account.

Bonus 1: Borrowing or lending money to family or friends could ruin relationships and friendships where one does not repay the family member or friend. In my opinion, if you do decide to lend money to someone, do it in small amounts that can easily be written off if it is not paid back. In that way, you will not be dependent on the reimbursement, and you will have a great excuse to not lend money to the same individual again.

4. Having a business can affect your home purchase decision. Some folks build their businesses first, then buy a home after;

> others do it the other way around. Consider starting a small business based on a hobby or something you enjoy the most. Give your business a name, register that name and create a professional social media account with that name. Maybe register the website via an internet service provider. If you can't think of a name, create a website in your name. The reason why this is important is that you can start to build a following, a network. If you don't have anything to sell or a service to provide, you can write blogs, start a podcast or do something to show your personality. If you already have a social media account, keep your personal account for personal posts and create another 'professional' account for business-worthy content. These days, employers check potential employees' social media accounts, so it's essential to differentiate between the two.

So, back to the business idea. This has more to do with your mindset and commitment. There are many businesses that young entrepreneurs start, for example, designing and selling T-shirts, making candles, washing cars, tutoring, mowing lawns, babysitting, baking cupcakes, acting, singing, playing an instrument and so on. Starting a business can be very inspiring. Create a business plan because if it doesn't work out now, it could work out in the future, but at least you would have made a start. Eventually, you will need to file taxes, but not until you are no longer being claimed as a dependent on your parents' or guardians' tax documents. Having a small business will help you write off a percentage of some of your expenses, such as your phone, a car note, gas, mileage, and internet.

Be cautious, though, because sometimes young entrepreneurs are helped financially by their parents, relatives, savings or inheritance. Don't be fooled by what you hear and see on social media, with social media influencers becoming rich overnight by selling their items on TikTok or other social media platforms. There have been many inspiring stories, but you have to do your research first, and it's OK to ask as many questions as you like until you're comfortable. Yes, it is true a lot of social media influencers are successfully getting residual income from their small businesses online, but not everyone.

It should also be something you're passionate about. People turn their hobbies into a business, and that often pays off. You may have seen many social media posts, reels, or stories of other young entrepreneurs who make their marketing videos look spectacular to drive more sales and have us, the viewers and listeners, click for more. That's called clickbait, where the main purpose of the marketing clip or sizzle is to attract attention and encourage us to click on a link to a particular webpage. All that glitters is not gold, meaning that not everything that looks true turns out to be so. In other words, because someone has done something and they say they are making money doing it, it doesn't mean they didn't suffer at one time in their life and had to bounce back. They may have failed initially and had to pivot a few times before success.

Being educated will help you understand the numbers, the financials, the marketing, and the ways to scale to make your business successful. You still need to be on top of your schoolwork (if you're still at school) or just on top of all your responsibilities. Once you're out of school, you will already have some kind of business or business mentality, which you can scale when you go to college or higher education.

5. Although whether you go to college does not affect your purchasing of a home or financial success, it could prevent you from getting a home purchased sooner rather than later.

College or university may not be for everyone, but if you are passionate about learning, you should try your best to complete higher education after your core school years. Completing college has many advantages; for example, it shows commitment, dedication and focus on a particular area of study. Completing college prepares you for the workforce and helps you network with other people and professionals.

One of the best reasons to go to college is that it teaches you how to think critically, how to research, solve problems, multi-task and to communicate effectively. Four years is actually a short time as it goes by very quickly, and when it's time for graduation, it becomes one of the best and most memorable days of your life. After putting in so much work, time and effort, you get the ultimate reward of graduating from college.

During college, start to build your resume or Curriculum Vitae. A resume is a formal document you create to itemize your qualifications and experiences for a particular role. It is a short account of your career, work ethic and qualifications to date. You may have held a job during your college years or outside of college, which will become part of your resume.

Your college years are an excellent time for utilizing many resources that can help develop your personal and professional skills. College offers much more than academic learning. It enables you to develop good interpersonal skills, time management and attention to detail. These are all vital skills essential for success in any career or industry.

Meeting new people from all over the world is another advantage of going to college. International students or student exchange programs are available at some colleges, depending on the course of study. It helps you to embrace diverse people, thinking and styles. You may also get the opportunity to travel abroad whilst at college.

Bonus 2: Apply for your passport now…or, if you already have a passport, ensure it is always valid with at least six months of validity as you cannot travel abroad if it doesn't have at least six months left.

I firmly believe they should teach life skills in school as a core subject. Life skills at the middle and high school level will set your children up for success. Getting on the right path early is crucial for your sanity and survival in the real world. Leaving school with a resume helps to see at a glance, what achievements you have accomplished thus far. It will help you to land your first job and build on it when and if you go to college or seek further education. You may have achieved some working or voluntary skills in school, which can act as experience and in addition to some transferable skills. Nowadays, you don't have to leave home to work or be employed; there are many home-based or remote jobs in fields like social media management, customer service and information technology.

To conclude, please remember that information is critical...you don't want to freely give information, especially personal information, out on social media. Treat social media like a public billboard in the palm of the hand, everybody's hand, so be careful what you disclose publicly.

At present, with so many social media sites, they are constantly finding ways to pivot so that people will continue to use the applications (apps) and keep posting valuable information for free. However, some social media sites help you monetize your content, so you can now start to benefit financially. We live in a world where the culture is to share anything and everything and, in return, receive likes, comments, and feedback. This culture is not going anywhere soon. It is here to stay, so you must learn to embrace it and not over-share online. If you can make some residual income with your social media content, go for it. Why not?

Remember when I said earlier that time is money, time is valuable…well, you can always make more money if you lose money, but you can never make up time when you waste it doing something that is not beneficial to you.

Not setting yourself up now for the future can cost you later with time, which you will not be able to get back. Spend your time (and money) wisely.

ABOUT CAROLINE BARROW

Ms. Caroline Barrow (a.k.a. *Cazzy Bee*) is a British native of Guyanese descent residing in Atlanta, Georgia. She embodies professionalism and has a wealth of expertise in account management, marketing, human resources, compliance, and travel. Throughout her corporate career, she has always managed to master a work-life balance by focusing on her goals while juggling motherhood, philanthropy, volunteering, helping and supporting others within her community.

She graduated with honours from the University of West London with a Bachelor of Arts in Business Management.

She has since worked for many international companies in the aviation, travel, media, and staffing industries. Having lived in three countries on three continents, she is an avid world traveller who can effortlessly connect with people of all cultures. She loves all things Caribbean, including the food, weather, music and entertainment. She was crowned Ms. Guyana UK 1997 and continues representing her heritage and love for Guyana at every opportunity.

She is the curator, executive producer and host of two weekly shows: *The Promo Show with Cazzy Bee,* which was created to help small businesses market and promote their products and services following the pandemic and *The Lunch Date with Cazzy*, a talk show with compelling conversations, insights, and wisdom from global influencers. She is also on the executive team at a local Community TV/Radio network in Atlanta, GA, and has successfully spearheaded the annual Community Day & Business Expo for the company for the last three years.

She received the 2023 Atlanta Caribbean Community Award for service in the TV/Radio category and was nominated for the 2024 Visionary Award in the "Woman on Fire" Network.

Writing and journaling have always been one of her passions, and as such, she is a co-author of two previous anthologies. She created a Career Advancement Training course for her consultancy and coaching business, which helps unemployed individuals and job hunters learn how to navigate and land the jobs of their dreams. She teaches her clients how to set themselves up for success, whether it be through promotion, a new job, a change in career, or networking.

She is a licensed Realtor in the State of Georgia with Century 21 Connect Realty, specializes in New Construction, and is a Georgia Property Management expert.

Contact Information and Social Media:
E: caroline.vaughncooke@gmail.com

THE PROMO SHOW
with CAZZY BEE

IG: https://www.instagram.com/the_promo_show/

YT: https://www.youtube.com/@catchthebuzzz

FB: https://www.facebook.com/cazzybeebee

From Silence to Strength: A Journey of Resilience and Advocacy

Annette Eberhart

When I was a young girl, I was quiet and reserved. I remember times when my mother's friends asked if I spoke. Most of the time, I watched and listened to everything around me. I can still remember when I'd hear a motorcycle, train, or construction; it was as if I could feel the sounds vibrating deep in my soul. I would cry and clasp both hands over my ears. When the noise stopped, I would slowly release my hands. This went on for several years until I eventually had surgery to correct the inflamed adenoids causing this disturbance. After having the surgery, I would still cover my ears when I heard loud noises. My subconscious remembered to react and protect. I outgrew the response to cover my ears, but I never became comfortable having conversations and being open with people other than my immediate family.

As I reflected on this time, it was as if I was crouched down inside, looking up to see if I could take a stand and show some expression. This lack of self-confidence began to affect my social life and my education. I recall when my mother was asked to come to my school to discuss my academic progress. I was being bused several miles away from home for school. My mother used public transportation, as she never had a driver's license, so we never had a car.

I still remember my kindergarten teacher, Mrs. Sawyer. She was an older woman with little patience, and I pushed the letter daily. There were times when Mrs. Sawyer would call on me to participate in an activity, and I would have this blank stare with no response. Inside, the little girl crouched down inside, was thinking, *why are you putting me on the spot in front of everyone? What if I say the wrong thing?* The more Mrs. Sawyer called on me, the more I would rebel. I began to act out, disrupting the class as my way of expressing my social-emotional insecurities. In the 1970s, inclusion wasn't accepted. It was looked upon negatively.

When I was a child, you went to school and did what you were told. Children didn't have much choice of expression. During the parent-teacher conference, I remember my mother looking down at me with concern as Mrs. Sawyer described my behaviour during class. There was discussion about placing me in a learning environment where I'd receive more one-on-one attention in Special Education (S.E.). My mother refused the suggestion and advocated on my behalf. She asked the principal and Mrs. Sawyer to give me some time so she could work with me at home.

Over time, I began to accept the world around me. The quiet time I spent listening and watching other interactions didn't seem as overwhelming. My mother would give me an extra hug and affection when she could to help me feel more secure. The world can be scary for a child who may be a little delayed in adapting to social norms. Parents are children's first teachers because parents provide care, love, and protection. This role is fundamental for brain development, helping to build the child's understanding of the social-emotional, cognitive, and physical world. Cultural upbringing can sometimes conflict with social expectations, leaving children vulnerable and confused about where or how they fit in.

During a transitional period in my life at the age of sixteen, I began to have an interest in the practice of Islam. I was attracted to the mysticism of it all, and I started to ask lots of questions about everything I had been taught to believe about spirituality/religion. Muslims were very popular in the 1980s and 1990s, and various sects were present up north in Connecticut and New York. After spending most of my teenage years trying to fit in, I searched for inner peace and fought for acceptance from my peers. The wrong look or feeling of rejection proposed toward me would cause an instant defensive reaction. The reaction varied based on the level of offence taken. I was known in my city, Stamford, for being a fearless fighter. The need to protect the little girl crouched down inside was my goal.

I was a senior in high school when I converted to Islam and became a Muslim, which raised lots of concerns at my school. I was once a troubled teen fighting my peers to become a fully Muslim young woman, fully veiled. My new goal became connecting with my new Islamic family.

Before I was eighteen years old, I moved into an Islamic community. I was married and pregnant with my first child, who was born before I was nineteen. I lived in the Islamic community for the next fifteen years, with people from all walks of life, each searching for their own inner peace. We all lived for, of, and by one another.

My husband and I were both teachers at the time. I taught the young girls from three to five years old, and he taught the young boys. I would give each child the same love, affection, and time I'd give my children. We taught the values and principles of life based on the Holy Quran and other Holy Tablets. My husband and I learned Arabic and could read, speak, and write it well. Our children's first language was Arabic. Our children were raised in a community environment away from any outside influences that would be a distraction from their Islamic path. Islam is a lifestyle; we embrace everything about it in the most peaceful way imaginable.

In 1993, we moved to Tampa, Florida. By this time, I had my second child, a son, born in Atlanta, Georgia, in

1990. By now, with several moves to various communities and having a collective of experiences, my then-husband and I were now administrators. With this role came lots of responsibilities and unwanted stress. With the responsibilities and duties of administrating a community of diverse people, I began to question my values as a Muslim woman. I started asking myself what I wanted to do in life. How could I make an impact? Muslim women were seen but not heard. As an administrator, I spoke extensively about what was needed for our community to thrive. I was at a crossroads, never really giving thought to life outside the community. I was so focused on being the best Muslim woman I could be, depicting the many great women of the Holy Quran and Holy Tablets.

The more interactions I had with the outside world, the more I began to look into my well-being. I started paying attention to my inner desire for more. I felt like I had outgrown the community lifestyle. I had learned so much from so many men and women, including so much about religion and spirituality, that I was ready to show and experience the world. I realized I would always be connected to God and didn't necessarily have to live in the community.

I started conversing with my then-husband, and we both felt the same way. It was time for a change. After another two, maybe three years as administrators in the Tampa community, we decided to leave the Islamic community lifestyle. We decided to invest all we learned into our family, which at the time was two children, my daughter and son. This leap was both scary and exhilarating. Once we were on our own, we faced many challenges. The pressure of life on our own without the community's support caused division between us. At the time, we embraced a new way of life, each depending on the other for support, but we lacked the trust and emotional connection to know we would get through this transition. As a result, we decided it was best to separate. Realizing I was alone caused me to return to a familiar place. I saw myself crouched down inside. I needed to protect the little girl inside; my conscience reminded me she was still there. This little girl would be there for me anytime I wanted to call on her for support.

I started to blame myself for the many non-traditional decisions I made. I blamed my parents for allowing me to move into an Islamic community at such a young and impressionable age. I blamed my ex-husband for stripping me of my innocence and making me a mother so early in life. I was vulnerable and afraid.

My children struggled to adjust to society outside of the community. The children in the community were like brothers and sisters—very close. My children were forced to learn the English language, which I'm sure was traumatic for them. The cultural shift was overnight, and it was a lot for them, along with their parents' separation. I was concentrating on surviving and my healing. I didn't know how to be the support my children needed.

I have learned that parenting doesn't come with a play-by-play manual. Parenting is a skill learned through cause and effect as well as experiences. The children eventually adapted to our new lifestyle. They were offered speech services in school, which significantly helped them. However, there was still a disconnect, with them not entirely fitting in for some time. Their names were not common, so they were wildly teased. I reassured them that things would improve over time, and they did.

In later years, I entered my purpose with grace and a strong passion for learning and giving. I am an educator who has faced and endured many transformational changes. Several experiences have taught me about trust, integrity, the importance of communicating your feelings and needs and knowing your value. Each of us chooses a path and has been given the ability to choose. I choose to be a voice for children when they cannot express themselves. I choose to be a voice for mothers who are trying their best within their power to model for their children. I choose to be a voice for mothers who are unsure of the value they bring to the world. I advocate for children who are delayed or have a unique need and require accommodations to be successful learners.

My experiences and involvement as an educator have made me see that we all learn as we grow. Your passion will be your prosperity once you connect with your true purpose. So here I stand, owner of a nationally accredited childcare program of seventeen years, Kidd's R Us F.C.C., L.L.C., which gave birth to Best Practices, a compilation of hands-on participation in shaping the minds of our youngest learners and researching best practices in the early learning profession.

Best Practices is a two-part series that is published and provides a blueprint for parents and educators to create positive and authentic relationships and interactions with children. Relationships are an essential part of children's development. The effects of a relationship can impact a child for life. Relationships shape the brain, creating connections to help children survive and thrive. Children who grow up without maternal or relationship support find it difficult to adapt to society.

The brain is a relational organ that needs input, connection, and sensory experiences. At Kidd's R Us, we service children from all walks of life. Inclusion is not a new term. It means accepting each child where they are tapping into their needs and building trust. As an educator, there is nothing like seeing that look of acceptance on a child's face when you've made a connection.

It's an honour to occupy the space I am currently in. I know and understand the importance of being present. Social-emotional dissonance is fundamental. Within the last few years, I have spoken to my peers about leadership and the need to make changes in our profession. I started taking on leadership roles, leading by example and attending college for higher education. I am a T.E.A.C.H. scholarship recipient through the Children's Forum in Florida. I received an AS degree in Early Childhood Education in 2022, graduating with high honours. I am currently enrolled at Rasmussen University, seeking a bachelor's degree in early childhood education - leadership with an expected graduation date of spring 2025. I have been on the dean's list twice during this journey and am president of the N.A.F.C.C. (National Association for Family Childcare) Accreditation Council. I serve on the Board of Directors as the provider representative for the Early Learning Coalition of Hillsborough County. I also serve as the Professional Development Coordinator for the Florida Family Childcare Home Association. Governor Ron DeSantis of the State of Florida appointed me to serve on the Interagency Coordinating Council for Infants and Toddlers. I am a mentor, workshop presenter, renowned author of three publications, public speaker, and the proud mother of three beautiful children who mean so much to me.

In 2018, I experienced a new love—like no other love I have experienced. I became a grandmother. Nova Gwyn was born on August 4, 2018. I remember it like yesterday, holding her in my arms for the first time after watching her enter the world. Sure, I'd had three children of my own, but witnessing a mother giving birth was life-changing in my eyes. This birth was special because she was of my bloodline. My son and his wife, together, made a beautiful new being. I saw Nova nearly every day. When she came of age, she started attending Kidd's R Us early education program.

I am grateful to participate in Nova's life and be a part of her experiences, moulding her to be the most excellent version of herself. I help Nova by allowing her to create, make mistakes, and experience her feelings. Communication is so essential. If children are uncomfortable communicating now, it will be even more challenging as adults. Becoming a grandmother has taught me patience and being present. I now know what I didn't know as a young mother and embrace being a grandmother. My path taught me integrity, accountability, spirituality, self-determination, and self-discipline. We live in a fast, technical society with distractions and attractions everywhere. It's not just the parents raising children. Societal influences are helping. Children gradually learn to identify how they fit into the world. Children are sponges, and they soak up everything around them.

In conclusion, I want Nova to always remember to choose happiness first and to understand that any room she walks into is a room she is meant to be in. By embodying self-confidence, she can silently communicate her worth and purpose, making a powerful impact without saying a single word. Her inner joy and confidence will light up any space, affirming her rightful place and presence.

ABOUT ANNETTE EBERHART

Annette Eberhart's unwavering dedication to early childhood education and advocacy is genuinely inspiring. With a wealth of experience and a heartfelt commitment to making a difference, she considers herself fortunate to play various roles within the field.

Ms. Annette Eberhart, the Owner and Director of Kidd's R Us Family Childcare LLC, is not just a caregiver but a passionate advocate for children. She teaches parents and caregivers how to empower their children to become the best version of themselves. Her advocacy work, spanning seventeen years in the ECE profession, has led to a new series of books titled *Best Practices for Parents*, inspired by her unwavering belief in children's potential. These efforts create an everlasting bond between parents and children of all ages, ensuring their well-being and development.

Annette has had the privilege of contributing to the NAFCC Accreditation Council as an author and educator, ensuring that the highest standards are upheld in early childhood care and education. Annette's involvement with the Florida Interagency Coordinating Council for Infants and Toddlers allows them to shape resources and policies that directly impact the development of the youngest learners.

In Annette's role as the Provider Representative for The Early Learning Coalition of Hillsborough County, they advocate for the needs of educators and families, striving to create a supportive environment for all. Additionally, as the Professional Development Coordinator for the Florida Family Childcare Home Association, Annette is dedicated to equipping early educators with the resources they need to be successful.

Beyond these roles, Annette is known for her innovative speaking engagements, sharing insights and best practices for promoting positive interactions between children and adults. Annette's advocacy work extends into the community, where they advocate for educational tools and resources for children, educators, and families, ensuring their voices are heard and their needs are met.

In everything they do, Annette is driven by a profound commitment to nurturing the well-being and development of future generations.

www.kiddsrus.org
www.kiddsrusfamilychildcare.com

Seeds of Wisdom for Tomorrow's Garden

Andrea Wardsworth Beasley

"Fear no thunder and run like a stallion in a green open pasture of sunshine or rain! Which stallion would you prefer to see running through your green pasture—a black or white one? Does it *really* matter to you? This is what I mean. *Continue to ask your questions. Learn. Grow. Allow your elders to help guide you in planting your garden!*

Parents, I ask that you be more open as an active listener and respond to your child's questions when they ask, **"Why?"** I have been a Louisiana Realtor for over twenty years and a retired Educator for over twenty-three years. I know that your kids are just trying to learn how *you* think. They want to understand *your* logic and reasoning and then mix them with their own thoughts before taking action. As I speak personally and professionally to you, my children and grandchildren, the most important ingredient to a successful life is *you*, so stay up for the "C" in Challenges so you can make an "A+" in your *life*! I am so full of warmth and nostalgia, thinking about the many good and bad adventures I have encountered. I remember some outstanding life lessons offered to me during high school, college, and my young adult years that I want to share with you as a newly seasoned grandparent. I pray that some of my "Seeds of Wisdom" are rooted within your spirit, body and mind. May my written words help you navigate this wild and wonderful world. Face your fears!

I ran out of my new coffee, which I recently discovered on the Internet. It contained less caffeine and mushrooms and was noted to be better for your digestive system. Then, my husband surprised me, as I discovered a new package of that coffee I had run out of in the cupboard yesterday. I sat down today and sipped on a second cup of my new favourite mushroom coffee with complete joy, as that warm cup of coffee comforted me for this challenge to write my current story tidbits today. Now, I am so full of warmth and nostalgia, thinking about the many good and bad adventures I have encountered.

Life is too short to be taken seriously *all the time*, but *life* has a way of grabbing your *attention* from time to time, so get up and try, try, try again and again! *Do not put yourself in a position to have to apologize. Look at every moment as a fresh beginning. Be you and do you. My youngest son would say, "Do Better." Do your best today to prepare for tomorrow.* Cry if you must when it is time, and then laugh even more. Just know this is my standard: Life will also try to move you backward periodically, so *smile.* I went to college to obtain a Bachelor of Science (BS) in Business Administration as a Major and Merchandising and Entrepreneurship as a Minor, so my insights will compare life to food and business—my two favourite things.

Life is like a busy marketplace full of sights, sounds, smells, and tastes that can overwhelm you and delight you all at the same time. Embrace any chaos that life may throw at you, like a crowded shopping centre. Form an image of the sounds of all the vendors calling out the items they have to sell and the vivid colours of the fruits, spices, clothing and all kinds of different people shopping at once in the marketplace. Things may get chaotic at times, but take a deep breath. Remember that the best treasures may be found in the most unexpected places, even in your spouse! For instance, my loving second husband whisked me off my feet and moved me from the central south part of Louisiana to the top northeast of the United States. God is good all the time! I did not know my new husband was up there waiting for me. I did not know until I ran across one of his sisters that he was still interested in me and had been since high school. Then he started flying down by way of the airport to see me, just as God whispered to me and told me he would.

Serving God promotes spiritual growth. It is like drinking a glass of water when you are thirsty. It is like a tree reaching toward the sun through the blue sky to grow stronger over the years of its existence. I am here to tell you that I was really needy and thirsty when I found God for myself. I cried out to God in my bed one day, looking for a change in my life during my first marriage because I wanted *out* of that marriage. I truly received the Holy Spirit lying in bed! My stomach deflated, and then the breath of God seriously inflated my body. When I got up from that bed and started walking, it felt like I was floating on air! I am delighted to mention that God is my foundation and "Plan of Action" for all things in life now. God is clearly my full meal ticket! He is my perfect picture example of *real love* and will always be at the forefront of my view because He has always found a way to show up for me to nourish my soul and give me strength to continue to *live* even during my depressing times. After all, He died for us so we can be more balanced, whole, and a better people.

I will continue to serve Him for the rest of my life on Earth *and in Heaven*. Set aside some time in the mornings and nights to pray. Start praying for three to five minutes. Hear the birds sing and wake up to the world with meditation. Live your faith and let your actions speak and reflect your beliefs. Be kind, compassionate, and honest. You need to nourish others just as the bread you eat and the water you drink nourish your body. A warm hug or hello goes a long way, too, so when others see you coming, they will smell your pleasing aroma from God! Find a good church community to help you continue to nourish you by providing support, love and a sense of belonging. We must receive the Holy Ghost to enter God's Kingdom. "Very truly I tell you, no one can enter the kingdom of God unless they are born of water and the Spirit." (John 3:5 [NIV])

Love reminds me of a flavourful potluck dinner. Everyone is supposed to bring something to the dinner table with a mix of recipes and flavours. You may be surprised sometimes. Seek advice from God about everything! Just be your authentic self in any relationship; the right person will love you and learn to love you and your different flavours. Learn to communicate and share clearly. You must learn to listen well to keep your communication open. Think of your love and time together being harmonious, like playing two different instruments that come together to make a smooth, melancholy sound. Have fun together by going on adventures. Attempt to talk about sex to your parents *first* before you start dating and having sex to hear *their* experiences, if you can, and if your parents are willing to talk about it. When you have a mate or spouse, definitely talk about the things you like regarding sex. You should do some self-exploration first so you can share more precise and intimate details with your spouse.

Feel the warm sand in between your toes. Break the routine of eating oatmeal for breakfast every day, although it is healthy. Spice things up sometimes! Try shrimp with grits or an egg omelette with sausage or turkey, spinach, onions, peppers and cheese. My husband occasionally surprises me by cooking breakfast, and I love his fluffy, yellow scrambled eggs. Lord, those are my favourites for breakfast, and it makes me feel special. "Dear friends, let us love one another, for love comes from God. Everyone who loves has been born of God and knows God. Whoever does not love does not know God, because God is love. (1 John 4:7-8 [NIV])

Marriage is like a delicious gumbo. Each spouse involved will add his or her own flavour over time. After the food simmers, you can taste the goodness. Look beyond the surface of the person and pay attention to small details with eagle eyes. How does that person communicate with others? Meet the parents and see how the family shows love towards one another. True love is similar to peeling the layers of a sweet purple onion and seeing a person's core. Marriage is a long road trip with your favourite person and life-long friend. Realize there will be wrong turns and pit stops along the way. As we age, due to body aches and pain, one spouse may become more grouchy and angry over the years. You may question your personal GPS and wonder if this was the right person, but you should still try to enjoy the journey. Be in a happy place. Let God be your guide. Seeing your other half happy and comfortable should make you happy, as you provide comfort! Marry someone who makes your heart sing, not just good eye candy. You will need to get on the "two-seated" bicycle provided and pedal together during your marriage.

Sometimes, one person takes his or her foot off the metal of the pedal, and then the other may have to pedal a little harder than the other one but enjoy the journey. Keep the romance alive! Touch. Continue to go on dates like it was the first time to keep that spark aflame! Add a little more effort to stir in more seasoning to add a lot more flavour to your gumbo pot. Surprise them with little gestures and more time together. "Two are better than one because they have a good return for their labor: if either one of them falls down, one can help the other up. But pity anyone who falls and has no one to help them up." (Ecclesiastes 4:9-10 [NIV])

Find and make laughter! You must find something to laugh about and laugh often! Imagine the laughter of friends sharing a meal even when you are alone or feel alone. Watch a funny movie or recall a silly memory. Laughter should be like the aroma of a fresh piece of warm bread or pies in the bakery I smelled years ago. Add some comfort to your soul. Gosh, I still love bread!

I narrowed my bread eating to one slice a week. However, everything we do seems to taste better with food if we stay within the right mindset. Do not overeat! I was a chubby-cheeked young girl as a child because of the bread I ate. I would eat four slices of bread per meal.

I also had shoulder-length straight hair when pressed with a straightening comb by my auntie in my grandma's kitchen, and I wore glasses. Lord, I can smell my hair burning from that heated iron. I also wore long white knee socks above my knees with dresses. I am laughing now because, in my youth, I wanted to make bread and give the loaves away to people wrapped in a scripture as my ministry. My sister knew my desire to make homemade bread and bought me a brand-new bread maker. Then we had a house fire, and the fire took everything we owned as our possessions went up in flames, along with my new bread maker! I never had an opportunity to use it.

I am the mother of five children who made significant attempts to help my family, as a single divorced mom, survive the elements of life, and we did. Life was so hard, yet I am so elated that I did it! I am still smiling! So, watch a movie in bad times and laugh at the absurdity of it all. Once you are a mother or father, you will always want to be a loving parent supporting your children to succeed and grow up until death. "So I commend the enjoyment of life because there is nothing better for a person under the sun than to eat and drink and be glad. Then joy will accompany them in their toil all the days of the life God has given them under the sun." (Ecclesiastes 8:15 [NIV])

Stay curious. Picture a child discovering the world and all its sounds for the first time. Can you see how wide their eyes open? Stay curious! Curiosity is the "Spice of Life." Ask questions, explore new things and never stop learning. I love what education and knowledge can bring to any table anywhere all over the world. Learn a new language! I still want to learn Spanish. Many have died and struggled to bring you the freedoms that you enjoy today, regardless of race. Learn your family traditions and celebrate all the talents and honours achieved by members of your own family. Recognize them. If you do not find any, be the *first* in your family to be recognized with Honours! Find your passions and get a good job. Learn from all those interpersonal and intrapersonal experiences at work with co-workers and tasks given to you by your supervisor.

Again, I say pay attention to small details! Work hard and smart, but do not let work consume you. Efficiency is your friend. Prioritize your task, delegate when you can, and use the tools you learn to streamline the tasks you have to perform. Work is like a strong cup of coffee; invigorating and sometimes a bit bitter, but hang in there! Do not quit unless you have something lined up to replace that missing income if you quit a job. Even if you are married, having your own money is a *good thing* to help you stay in control of yourself as much as possible. No matter how great your spouse seems to be at the time, this is a good thing. Remember, sometimes the mind changes for whatever reason. Sharing wealth and supporting one another is the best way to handle money for all parties involved to reach a common goal *faster.* When you find your passions, you have the energy to continue going to work because it excites you and makes you want to get out of bed each day. Keep your dreams alive! You may not get your dream job right away, but it will come. In the meantime, get a job and keep a job to survive and pay your way to achieve future goals and become more independent. Remember that you must balance work and play. Do not become so consumed with work or starting a business and not have time to drink some good Country Time lemonade, my favourite, and then spend time with family and friends and have fun. “The heart of discerning acquires knowledge, for the ears of the wise seek it out.” (Proverbs 18:15 [NIV])

School can be a great experience! It is not always about grades; however, you need to get good grades to graduate successfully within a certain period. Graduate from school and allow that education to help your life’s journey become brighter and more apparent. Stay focused! Keep your eyes on your path ahead with your written goals. Distractions may come to lead you astray, but stay the course and make good connections.

Good connections are like birds chirping in the trees to me every morning. God, I love to hear the birds sing! Can you hear how they sing and talk to one another? Well, you need to build good relationships with classmates, professors, teachers, and other professionals who come across your path. I told my children to ask for and keep the phone numbers and emails of all who are instrumental in their lives. You never know whom you will need to call down the road to help or who can help you. I also asked them to walk up to their teachers on the first day or week of school to introduce themselves and ask, “How can I make an A in your class?” I could tell when they did not do it because I wondered where their A's were! They were missing! Although I joke about their lack of A's, honestly, they were all *"Honour Roll students."* Anyway, it is all about great networking and making a significant impact on the world. "I can do all this through him who gives me strength." (Philippians 4:13 [NIV])

Choose your friends wisely. Friends are like a pair of jeans or shoes. It may be hard to find a good fit sometimes, but when you find an excellent pair to fit, they are with you for life! It is important to have good friends in school, church, or the community to attend events until you find your spouse. They teach us socialization skills at a young age. I cannot stress this enough! It is better to have a few good friends who enrich your life instead of a large group that adds *no real value*! Remember that a good "real" friend will support, encourage and bring out the best in you. A good friend can be like a favourite warm, soft blanket. They should be supportive, reliable, honest, and willing to share their time and lend a hand. Friends are there through thick and thin. Stay in touch to keep good friendships alive with a call, visit, pictures, or "Hello" text. A unique joy comes to your life from helping, serving and sharing with others. You should be able to recognize the positive changes you help bring forth with friends and your community together. Join some organizations! "Be very careful, then, how you live—not as unwise, but as wise, making the most of every opportunity, because the days are evil." (Ephesians 5:15-16 [NIV])

Making money is like planting seeds; save some and give it time to grow! Try to set a portion aside to grow before you spend it on big items. Weed your "Money Garden" and get rid of debts that can choke you financially. We all have to obtain credit cards to establish a credit history and a good credit score. This is the way of the world now. You cannot buy a house or a car without good credit unless you are fortunately *born* into a wealthy family who can give you the cash to make a purchase today. You are entitled to enjoy the fruits of your labour sometimes. Be cautious of overspending! Experiences do create memories. You need to travel periodically and learn new skills to enrich your life for the years to come. You may become a grandparent one day, and you need stories to tell them. Learn to invest as well. "Honor the Lord with your wealth, and the first fruits of all your crops; then your barns will be filled to overflowing, and your vats will brim over with new wine." (Proverbs 3:9-10 [NIV])

In conclusion, *life* can be a tremendous, incredible *journey* full of patterns and turns that offer much to your senses of sight, sound, smell and taste. Through it all, continue to keep a smile on your face and love in your heart. Embrace the challenges and cherish the good moments. You may not understand now when others say, "Life is too short," but the years will creep up on you. Your bones may start to pop, and you will feel discomfort, so visit your dentist and doctor. Brush your teeth three times a day. Sip a glass of your favourite wine when you are of age. Stay healthy! Time does not stand still. Seize your opportunity to serve God with a joyful heart, show and receive love, get educated, work smart, choose your friends wisely, and then save some room for your favourite dessert as you navigate your ride through your life! Keep your sense of wonder and bewilderment.

I hope that my "Seeds of Wisdom" continue to bless you and help you find your way with some humour and a lot of heart. I am outstretching my open arms to you in an extended position like an olive branch. I am only a phone call away. My life is an open book like the "Show and Tell" of time well spent toiling away in the rich soil with my hands to make my garden grow to a gorgeous blood-red-orange flowering bloom that I love to see.

You are one of my blooms! I LOVE YOU! *I honour you*! *I honour you for being a part of my life! You are one of God's blessings. You are a survivor.* I give you my blessing to spread your wings and fly before the open golden blue skies. Before you get to be my age of almost sixty-five, always remember that LIFE IS SERIOUSLY TOO SHORT! In addition, life is what you make it because you are the key. I will be here to guide you into your tomorrow as long as our God allows me to be. This is our legacy. I send you much love and laughter. *Have hot fun in the summertime and smile!*

ABOUT ANDREA WARDSWORTH BEASLEY

Andrea Wardsworth Beasley is an innovative author born in Louisiana. She is the first-born of two children and is of Native American descent. Prior to her writing career, Andrea and her five children walked away *alive* from a house fire disaster! After fighting for survival, she received a Master of Arts in Teaching degree on her fiftieth birthday, December 12, 2009, from Louisiana Christian College in Pineville, Louisiana. Andrea also attended the University of Louisiana in Lafayette, where she obtained her degree in Business Administration.

Andrea pens about real life, often in fiction, and describes her traumatic, pleasant, and aha moments, explaining her loves and fears through writing. She believes that most trials and errors pull a person into another dimension for dreams and visions to be brought to reality and shared with the world. She loves writing poetry and inspiring others by making life come alive in her books. Andrea's Great Spirit of Understanding sets her apart, making her a "writing paradigm" for capturing the essence of life's troubles and triumphs. She dedicates most of her books to her children, who have stood by her side through the most critical years of single parenthood.

She started her writing career by collecting the pieces of her life, one book at a time. There was little time to relax or think about being a single divorced mother of five, a Christian, a Veteran in the Army, a twenty-four-year Teacher, an Instructional Facilitator, and a Louisiana Realtor. Andrea recently retired as a teacher and married her new husband, Charles, at the beginning of her retirement.

Andrea's writings are "Refreshing to the Mind and Soul." Andrea's books include themed preschool tracing and handwriting books, a children's story with a separate activity book titled *Ayanna Loves Loves Domino*, and a children's book called *My Mamma Got Freaky Hair,* about a mom with cancer. She has also written self-improvement guides, including *Connections Until We Part to Another Life,* about differences between Trust and Wills, and *HEALED! A Personal Food and Medical History Record*, a holistic approach to diet and food intake, *Up Close Because of You Journals,* and a memoir about the fire disaster, *A Fire Arose from My Soul: A Memoir of Faith.*

Andrea continues to share her Vision from God for her love of educating children by expanding the arts and literacy in unique ways!

Website: https://www.aroseenterprisesllc.com/

Embracing the Unexpected: How Setbacks Can Be Setups for Something Better

Dawn James

Life is like a jigsaw puzzle. We arrive here with a box full of pieces, but no one gives us the lid. So, we scratch our heads and try to figure it all out. Sometimes, we get lucky and pick out two pieces that fit together just right. However, more often than not, it takes a series of trials and errors to get things to fit together. Imagine if we had a lid for that jigsaw puzzle box and knew where all the pieces went. That would make life seem easy and probably very boring. Life is designed to be a journey of experiences, insights and discoveries. Sometimes, we walk it, trip over it, make a U-turn or get bumped off the road entirely! Now and again, everyone encounters setbacks. When a setback occurred in my youth, I would instantly ask—*why me, why now*? However, as I got older and hopefully a little wiser, I began to reflect on *where and how*—where is the blessing or opportunity in this setback? How is this setback causing me to shift, change, grow, and release?

Physical Disabilities Brought Me New Gifts

I have experienced more than my fair share of setbacks that became progressively more intense as I became an adult. In my childhood, I experienced several physical disabilities—some were explainable, and some were not. For instance, I lost my hearing for three days when I was seven years old. The doctor could not explain it; however, when my hearing returned—with it came empathic abilities. I began to feel what others were feeling. I could sense when people were in pain physically or emotionally. I could also feel their fears and their joys. When my hearing returned, it marked the start of my journey of understanding and embracing compassion for others. These new gifts served me well throughout my life.

I started playing piano when I turned nine. After only six months of taking lessons, my teacher convinced my parents that I was ready for my first piano recital. I did not even know what a recital was. No one explained that I would walk into a room with over 200 people, and three judges would be at the stage looking and listening to me while I played the piano. I was used to coming home from school and sitting on the bench playing for an hour or two. I loved music and loved to perform. However, on the day of my first piano recital, when I entered the huge lecture hall at our local university, I became extremely nervous and anxious. OK, let's be honest; it was total stage fright. I looked around the room, and there were so many people. My hands started to heat up, and the top of my head also got warm. Then I noticed the room seemed cloudy. By the time the judges called my name, the room was dark grey and turning quickly to black. I barely managed to walk across the stage to sit on the bench. My heart was racing! I placed my two hands on the keys, and everything turned *black*. I saw no one and nothing, just black.

I lost my vision temporarily for twenty minutes (just as I sat at the bench, getting ready to play). A little voice inside me helped me calm down when I heard, *"You do not need eyes to see."* Ironically, I felt a little relieved when I could not see anyone or anything. I pretended I was playing blindfolded and just concentrated on what I had practiced over and over again. To my surprise and delight, I played my piece to perfection, trusting in that little voice. Little did I know my nervousness and anxiety were causing a phenomenon known as temporary blindness. My vision became stable when I stopped playing piano and ended my journey with the Royal Conservatory of Music at age nineteen.

What was the blessing of losing my vision?

I learned to trust myself and my musical abilities. Temporary blindness did not stop me from doing what I loved—playing piano. The confidence that grew within me from this setback spilled over into my academic life and, eventually, my career. I excelled in school, skipping three grades between ages nine and seventeen. Needless to say, I started university earlier than most and began working full-time at age twenty. Physical challenges in my youth taught me to become resilient and believe in myself.

A Christmas Shock and a New Year's Blessing

There is one Christmas holiday I will never forget. It was supposed to be a time of celebration and gathering with family and friends; however, the Universe had another agenda for my husband and me.

I was a bookkeeper at the time. We had a sixteen-month-old and were expecting our second child, due Christmas Day. It was mid-December, and I was home on maternity leave. My husband arrived home and told me the most terrible news—he was let go from his full-time job because of cutbacks. I had to ask him to repeat what he said because I thought I was dreaming when he first spoke. "Yes, it's true," he said, "but do not worry, things will work out."

It's human nature that when you hear the words "do not worry," you begin worrying. Here we were ten days before Christmas, two adults not working, with a toddler and one on the way. I tried to remain calm on the outside, but a storm of worry was brewing inside. It was a sombre Christmas Day with no signs that the baby was ready to arrive. In fact, I was not even getting contractions. More worry followed by a doctor's visit. The doctor echoed the same sentiment as my husband, "Do not worry, Mrs. James, the baby will be here soon." Our beautiful little girl arrived on New Year's Day five days later. Her big cheeks and bright smile melted my feelings of anxiety.

On January 3rd, I got a surprising phone call from a company where I had worked three years prior. They asked if I would consider working on a six-month contract to replace their Controller, who was going on a sabbatical. *Wait...what?* I asked them to repeat the question as I thought I was dreaming.

"Are you interested in a six-month contract as a Controller?"

I looked at the little baby curled up in my left arm. I replied in a calm voice, "Yes, I am," then quickly added, "When do you want me to start?"

"How soon can you start?"

They say honesty is the best policy, so I told them I had a newborn and asked if they would allow me to go home twice a day to nurse her. To my delight, they said *yes*. Four weeks later, I started working full-time as a Controller.

From my house to their office was a six-minute drive. I will forever be grateful for that New Year's blessing to be offered a job at a time when we were both unemployed with two young children. The second blessing was learning to be a Controller, responsible for a company's accounting and payroll functions. The Controller returned from a sabbatical and graciously gave me a glowing letter of reference, which allowed me to leave bookkeeping and start a new career in financial management.

Double Trouble - Two Car Accidents Six Months Apart

Do you ever feel your life is on a merry-go-round, and similar experiences keep happening to you? Like you find yourself in a job you dislike and leave it—only to find yourself in a similar job you dislike. Or you are attracted to a particular personality and keep meeting people with the same personality.

I experienced two car accidents exactly six months apart. The second accident changed the trajectory of my life in a profound way.

One sunny Spring day, I was driving to a job interview and waited at the intersection for the light to turn green. It was 8:20 a.m. When the light turned green, I made a right-hand turn, and then it happened. A car raced through the red light and clipped the front driver's side of my car. The impact spun my car around, making my body jolt and twist about (thank God for seatbelts). It was the first car accident I ever experienced. Needless to say, I never arrived at my interview.

My body was in bad shape, and I had several practitioners working with and on me—including a physiotherapist, masseuse, osteopath, and acupuncturist. Recovery came slowly, but it came.

Six months later, I was driving to another job interview. I had just filled my car with gas and was preparing to pull out of the gas station. It was 8:20 a.m. Out of nowhere, I saw a vehicle two car lengths in front of me with its reverse lights on. I honked my horn to notify him I was behind him. Instead, he revved his car and reversed swiftly, hitting the front driver's side of my car. It happened so quickly that I did not have time to place my car in reverse to avoid the hit. My body lunged forward and back as my neck braced for the impact. *What the hell!?* I was fuming mad—at the driver, the pain in my body, and the world. To add salt to my new wound, the driver sped off. Needless to say, I never made it to my interview. The gas attendant approached my car window to ask if I was OK. I nodded *no*, and they called an ambulance.

While I was sitting there in my car, the initial anger I felt began to dissipate. I realized the cycle had repeated, going to a job interview and never arriving, another car accident at exactly 8:20 a.m., and damage to my car in the exact location—front driver's side. My eyes opened wide, and I finally got the proverbial memo: *Dawn, you do not need a job; you need to do what you came here to do. Trust in your calling!*

I looked up and said, "OK, I hear you. Please stop hitting my car."

I learned a crucial lesson that day, sitting in my car waiting for the ambulance. The Universe was trying to get my attention on both occasions. I came to realize that sometimes the Universe gets our attention with a whisper (hunches, gut feelings, dreams), and other times the Universe will SHOUT to get our attention (car accidents, breakups, job losses, etc.) I needed a SHOUT to tell me I was heading onto the wrong path. A *day job* was not the place for me to find fulfilment and be in service to others.

Who knew it would take two car accidents for me to realize I needed to stop being an employee and become a business owner?

After my second car accident, I founded a company called Publish and Promote. My vision was to guide writers in finding their authentic voice and sharing their stories to educate and inspire others. I genuinely believe that by sharing our stories, we develop an appreciation and understanding of others, and sharing our journeys can make us more compassionate human beings. Managing Publish and Promote fulfilled my passion for teaching and mentoring others; the books we helped writers birth changed lives in so many wonderful ways.

Finding the Silver Lining in Setbacks

Setbacks can come in many forms: a job loss, unplanned or unwelcome changes, moving, loss of a loved one, financial loss, etc. You have heard about my major setbacks spanning four decades.

If we take the time to look at our setbacks with new eyes or from a higher vantage point, we may find some hidden gem, new knowledge, gift or blessing in that setback. One of the ways I began to realize the lessons in my challenges and setbacks was by journalling how I was feeling. I started to ask myself questions such as:

- *Where was the hidden blessing?*
- *Where was the lesson?*
- *How did this change me?*
- *How did this shift my perspective?*
- *How did this affect my personal or professional development (new learning, growth, release)?*

The more I wrote, the easier it became to make sense of it all. By asking self-reflection questions, I connected to my higher self, my inner guru, if you will. In time, I realized that the answers were within me all along. Journalling helped me see a glimpse of the proverbial lid of the jigsaw puzzle box of my life, if only for a moment.

ABOUT DAWN JAMES

Dawn James is the Founder and Managing Director of Publish and Promote, a company dedicated to teaching others "the business of being a successful author." Since 2010, she has coached hundreds of writers to fulfill their dream of becoming published authors. There is nothing quite like seeing your name in print. Dawn cherishes the relationship she builds with each of her clients in their quest to become published. Dawn is passionate about teaching others how to write for impact, leave readers turning the pages, and connect to their ideal audience!

Dawn is also an **international award-winning author** for her incredible afterlife story *Unveiled: Autobiography of an Awakened One* (2022 Silver Nonfiction Award | Reader's Favorite). In *UNVEILED,* Dawn shares her astonishing life and spiritual journey and strengthens her connection to a higher power, which was partly inspired by the health challenges and physical phenomena she faced as a child, including deafness, blindness, and paralysis. Several spiritual concepts are explained in *UNVEILED*, including Kundalini Awakening, Merkabah, Breatharians, Unity Consciousness, and Soul Mates.

Inspired to start writing by some encouraging words from the late Sylvia Browne, Dawn published the *Raise Your Vibration* trilogy, which teaches others to live mindfully and in harmony with each other and the planet.

Dawn is also the Founder of *For the Grandchildren*, an organization dedicated to collecting, preserving, and sharing Elder Wisdom for the betterment of future generations.

Today, she shares her knowledge and passion for teaching and mentoring through her books, workshops, Soulful Living Coaching program, The Right Place to Write Retreat, Beyond Your Book author training program, and her company Publish and Promote.

Connect with Dawn

www.dawnjames.ca
www.publishandpromote.ca
www.therightplacetowrite.ca
www.beyondyourbook.ca

From Parent to Grandparent - A New Joyful Role

Oluyinka Marcus

My dream of becoming a grandparent came true when my husband and I received a newborn "onesie" from our son and his wife with inscriptions revealing that we were grandparents. Words cannot express the indescribable joy of becoming a first-time grandparent. Then, another special announcement came a year later when our daughter shared her good news. I was filled with incredible joy! Knowing that I will be a significant part of these children's lives for the rest of my life to pass on a legacy that will continue for generations, was a beautiful dream come true. When the children you love have children of their own, it creates a unique and special love relationship. Becoming a grandparent is about getting to love on your children all over again and expanding your love capacity for the next generation.

The first time I held each of my grandchildren in my arms, it was like being gifted with precious jewels. I sang, danced and prayed as I welcomed them to this world, knowing that they would experience love and care from their parents and grandparents. It felt like I had empty spaces in my heart that needed to be filled, and they filled it perfectly. I would gaze into their eyes and wouldn't want to stop. I cherished those initial moments of bonding. I realize our bond gets stronger as I grow into my role. I never knew how meaningful my grandchildren's hugs, smiles and laughter would be until they hugged my neck with their little hands when they blew me kisses and laughed at gestures that I thought were insignificant. The only way I can describe this experience is that I am "being tickled." They are precious moments.

Grandparenting is a stage of life to be treasured, and it is a privilege and an honour. I would like to acknowledge God Almighty, The Giver of Life, Creator and Provider. Everything I have comes from Him. My

Christian faith has been my life, my strength and my hope. I was born into a Christian family, and being surrounded by Christian values is a cherished legacy. My childhood experience included frequent church attendance, during which I was blessed with several great role model "grandparents" (*non-biological.*) They were quite "grand" in their expressions of love.

These "grandparents" provided happy, unforgettable memories. For example, I never wanted to miss the children's church meetings led by "Mama Sunday" ("*mother of Sunday school*"), mainly because of her huge hugs and the warm, delicious snack called "*puff-puff.*" It was a special snack everyone liked. "Mama Sunday" was quite energetic and stern but gentle with children. She was very much loved. It was a delight to learn about the Bible, and the "*puff-puff*" was an incentive for attentiveness. Children tried to impress Mama Sunday by enthusiastically learning the Bible memory verses, singing all the songs loudly and participating in the Bible quizzes. I still remember those Bible verses and songs.

In my Nigerian Yoruba culture, everyone contributes to the raising of children. It really takes a village to raise a child! I thoroughly enjoyed the company and love of two exceptional "grandparents," my father's stepmother and his sister. My aunt was known for her very spicy food—delicious! I enjoy spicy food today because of her. Each visit from my step-grandmother was accompanied by a variety of gifts. She was a kind woman. My takeaway from my experience with them is that grandparenthood is about love and care through faith, kindness, spending quality time in play and laughter, and food.

My paternal grandmother and my maternal grandfather were exemplary. Although I was young, I remember the frequent visits to my grandfather, filled with joy, laughter, gifts and food. He was friendly and playful with his grandchildren. He would welcome us with such enthusiasm and joy. I enjoyed every welcome moment from him. At these visits, there was nothing much to do except sleep, eat and play, although grandparents would teach grandchildren house chores and other age-appropriate activities. My fondest memory of my grandfather was his smiles, gifts, and welcoming community. I remember looking forward to his hugs and generosity.

My grandmother was very kind, generous, soft-spoken, and hard-working, even in her old age. Living in the same city with her was a privilege as it enabled a more frequent visit. Her warm welcome with hugs and lovely traditional praise statements is known as "oriki." These statements, common with grandparents in my culture, describe ancestorial achievements and status, strengths and identity of our tribe and affirmations that spoke life and strength to someone's spirit. She would provide a sumptuous authentic dish known as "Àmàlà" (*a special meal made from African yam, served with unique sauces*). This delicacy has become my favourite dish.

From my childhood experience with my grandparents, I am connecting with my grandchildren through faith, kindness, quality time and food. The faith legacy (*or spirituality*) is an important aspect to pass on as it provides moral and life guidance. This is about grounding them in their spirituality and praying for them. My hope is that they will grow up with the conviction that God loves them and that spirituality is an important area of life. Showing and teaching kindness is an act of unconditional love where, for example, I hope to focus on their strength and speak affirmatively to them rather than stress on behaviour adjustments. I want to consistently reassure them that I will be there for them whenever they need guidance and comfort.

Spending quality time with undivided attention is another vital legacy. As a grandmother, quality time involves engaging with my grandchildren in the activities they are interested in, creating fun and great memories. My grandchildren, among other activities, love books and the outdoors. They have bookshelves built for them, and they pick out books to read, especially at bedtime. It is always fascinating to watch my first granddaughter pick book after book just for one bedtime reading. As early as nine months, the first recognized word for my second granddaughter was 'book.' When the word was mentioned, she would look up at the shelf of books and point at one of her favourites. They both enjoy opening books and following along with the reading.

I look forward to sharing my love of the outdoors with my grandchildren as they grow older, including hiking, taking walks, and visiting parks. The joyful moments of walking with my grandchildren to the community park were always great without the need to rush. It is important to be *present* with them and allow for frequent stops as they choose. In addition to sharing my love for the outdoors, sharing my favourite ethnic dishes with them is a meaningful feature of my grandparenting. They've enjoyed tasting some dishes, but others have not been their favourite. Somehow, I am convinced that they will grow to enjoy these meals. *No pressure.* I look forward to many more experiences around food.

My childhood experience with my non-biological grandparents confirms that grandparenthood is a role and a "positioning" where a recognizable opportunity is given to an older individual who impacts the little one's life with special friendship, love and care. Before becoming a biological grandparent, I played the role of a grandparent to several children and gained the nickname "Nana." I thank them all for giving me a memorable "grandparent" experience. I learnt from this experience the importance of non-biological grandparents who will fill the void in children's lives where biological grandparents are absent. It is always an opportunity to love and care for the next generation.

Becoming a parent is life-changing, and grandparenthood is transitioning into a transforming season of life. I get to joyfully rearrange my schedule to be there for my grandchildren. I find they are always on my mind when I am not with them. I remember being at an event and missing my granddaughter, who was at home. I wanted to get home to be with her. Saying goodbye is quite emotional after a visit, especially when your granddaughter cries when it's time to leave. I am grateful that technology has transformed how we relate and stay connected to our granddaughter. Since becoming a grandparent, I have learnt to be more gentle and patient and have become more tolerant.

I am thankful to my children for making me a grandparent and showing me some new ways of parenting. It has been a pleasure watching them love on their children and being generous with their time and energy. They read books, listen to podcasts and connect with other parents to gain knowledge for effective parenting. Since becoming a grandparent, I have realized that my tendency to "be in charge" and my effort to enforce my own perception based on my parenting experience will result in unnecessary power struggles with my children about their parenting. I am open-minded, and I appreciate their efforts. I trust them as parents, and I need to step back, respect and honour their decisions as the direct parents. It is becoming more meaningful to me that my grandparenting role is indeed an opportunity to be a parent again without making parental decisions.

I admire my children as they learn and share new ideas that are different from my parenting days. For example, I did not schedule naps for my children, I gave them water when they were less than six months old, and they did not sleep in separate bedrooms when they were babies. I realize that honouring them is more important than enforcing a tradition. I continue to admire all their efforts to learn from experts regarding the possible hazards of some of the "risky" practices I engaged in. With an open mind, I have joined in listening to parenting podcasts with my daughter, and she suggested reading up on "modern" parenting by "experts," although I hold different opinions on some of the views. I am learning to comply with the changing times as much as possible. I am grateful to experience this new perception of my children. I see them differently. They are wise and engaging parents. Without undermining my vast knowledge and wisdom, I've learned to ask my children how they would like things done for their children, even when I know what I can do.

Since becoming a grandparent, I have enjoyed reading books such as *Parenting in the Present Moment,* written by Carla Naumburg (2014). She rightly explained how effective parenting is not "...about directly controlling our child's behaviour..." (Naumburg 2014, 46), and her suggestion for parents to learn how to stay connected, grounded and present with their children is what I needed when my children were growing up. I grew up with the authoritarian parenting style, which was the standard approach where everything was about obedience, punishment and discipline. The focus was on controlling behaviour by any means possible, and parents were reactive. At a point in my parenting life, I realized I was quite a reactive parent. This realization led to some reconciling conversations with my children, and I began the journey of transformation to better relate with them. I have become more reflective. It is a joy to become more connected with my children through my interaction with their children.

Hunter Clarke-Fields' *Raising Good Humans: A Mindful Guide to Breaking the Cycle of Reactive Parenting and Raising Kind, Confident Kids* (2019) is the other book I like. He takes readers through various helpful tasks to enhance parenting. He encouraged parents to mindfully identify and meet their personal needs as much as possible for more effective parenting. As much as I consider myself a "good parent," I wish I had been less reactive, authoritarian and frustrated with my children.

As a grandparent, I engage with my grandchildren with patience, gentleness, and kindness. It's like becoming a parent again, but better.

In conclusion, as a grandparent (*biological or non-biological*), it is meaningful for me to keep loving my grandparents and pass on the legacy of faith, spending quality time and kindness, and sharing ethnic dishes with my grandchildren. It is essential for me to keep learning to enrich my relationship with my children, allow them to be parents, and avoid being controlling. I look forward to engaging in all kinds of other fun activities as my grandchildren grow older, offering support physically, emotionally and financially when needed, being there for them during their life's challenges, sharing their milestone achievements and joys, and providing protection when required. I see my children as wise parents, and I trust that they will become awesome grandparents as they continue to learn and be there for their children in every way. I hope they will pass on the legacy of faith, quality time, kindness and sharing their favourite ethnic dishes.

I am forever grateful to God for the privilege of grandparenthood, making a mark on these precious lives as I contribute to their growth through caring and providing life-changing experiences for the benefit of their generation and the generations to come. I pray that all my family and friends who are looking forward to becoming grandparents will be blessed soon. I treasure this stage of my life. I treasure my children and grandchildren as they continue to teach me how to be a grandparent. It's genuinely a treasured life.

ABOUT OLUYINKA MARCUS

Oluyinka Marcus, MA, is a certified professional counsellor in Calgary, AB, Canada. Oluyinka supports people in personal and relational wholeness, pre-marital and marital counselling, grief and trauma therapy, and spiritual wellness. She is on the board of directors of the Association of Counselling Therapists of Alberta, ACTA. Oluyinka's hobbies include dancing, singing, and hiking. She is a public speaker, a mentor and a co-author. She is married with two adult children and grandchildren. She is the founder of Hope Alive Counseling Services and Ministry, her private practice and not-for-profit organization (www.hopealive.ca).

An Invitation

Give the gift of wisdom to the next generation!

We invite you to share your story at
www.forthegrandchildren.org.

For the Grandchildren is a global community dedicated to collecting, sharing, and preserving stories from grandparents, seniors, and elders worldwide for the betterment of the grandchildren of today and the future.

Printed in Great Britain
by Amazon

46095462R00116